> *I write as I teach; I teach as I broadcast;*
> *I broadcast as I play; and I play when*
> *I feel I have something to share.*
>
> *–Gerry Brody*

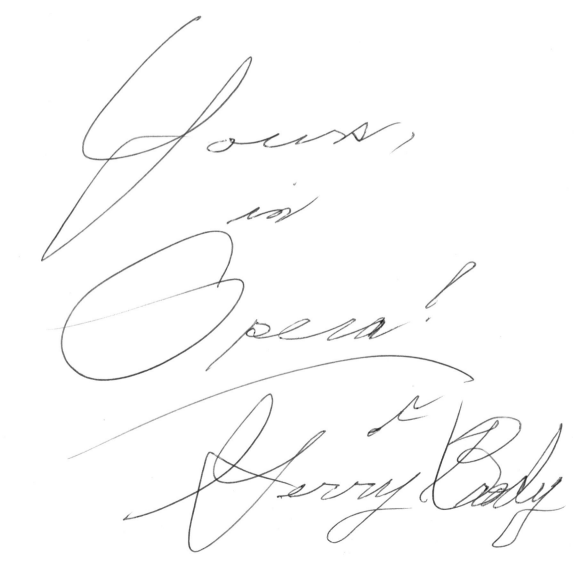

OPERA:

You Never Knew You Loved It!

Cover and original illustrations by Richard Zayac

Visit Gerry Brody's Website
www.operasregularguy.com

Published by

High Rose Publishing

in cooperation with

Trafford Publishing Trafford
PUBLISHING

ISBN: 978-1-4120-8994-4

Printed in Victoria, BC, Canada.

Note for Librarians:
A cataloguing record for this book is available from the Library and Archives Canada at: www.collectionscanada.ca/amicus/index-e.html

10 9 8 7 6 5

Acknowledgements

- Heartfelt thanks to that appreciative 'senior student' who felt "cheated" that *The Joy of Opera* was not syndicated nationally, and who asked– no, virtually demanded– that I do the "next best thing and write a book." Thanks to you, Sir, and a few others like you, I just did!

- Susan, please accept the "1st Annual 'Mother Theresa' Award" for your *JOBean* patience (see "Afterglow").

- Profound gratitude to my friend, the brilliant multi-faceted artist Richard Zayac. Dick "read my mind" after I initially expressed my general ideas for the cover and attendant sketches. Not one person who has seen the cover art has failed to laugh viscerally.

- Thank you, thank you, Pat Richter, for offering your professional expertise in providing *indexing* as a gift.

- *Grazie*, Scarlet Robbins for transforming my 19th century manuscript– but certainly not my mentality– into the required 21st century format. It was "no big deal" as you said, but as the legendary ventriloquist Senor Wences used to say: "For you *EEE-cee*, for me DEE-fee-cult!"

–G. M. B.

Note: Your author thinks, visualizes, and writes musically. Within this context, a decision was made to employ italicization somewhat beyond its standard usage in foreign language terms, titles of literary or musical works and a few other specific applications. In so doing, certain words and phrases intended for special emphasis will be italicized rather than, for example, enclosed by quotation marks which is felt to be more invasive to the visual and rhythmic flow of the meter in this effort.

TABLE OF CONTENTS

PROLOGUE

Music, from its nebulous beginnings, was felt to possess magical powers. The Bible relates the curative effects of David's harp and the wall shattering reverberations of Joshua's trumpet; yet, long before these instruments were made by man, there was the original creation– the human vocal cords. Sun, moon and star chants probably emanated from the throats of the first vertical Homo sapiens.

Since the subject of this book saw the light of day for the purpose of glorifying classic Greek drama, a most vital reality must always be kept in clearest perspective: before there was *poetry* and before there was *painting*, there was **song**. Homer was a *singer* and evidence points to him following a long line of kindred melodic historians. Since he was blind, the magnificent bard surely had scribes, using the newly invented Greek alphabet to transpose the historical songs into the written word. Thus, the seeds of two-thirds of what would be *opera* were already sown. How could Homer (born over seven centuries BC) have provided such exquisite detail about the legendary Trojan War, fought a full half millennium before, without any written roadmaps? The answer – *Song*! Songs passed down through countless generations. Songs, with background accompaniment of one of the two instruments of the day, the plucked *lyre* or the blown *aulos*. The first *aria* may well have been "Celeste Achilles."

In *Opera in the Twentieth Century**, Ethan Mordden succinctly elevates the unique vocal art form to the *Olympus* where it belongs in that "...now it seems that the lines of the Greek plays were sung, not spoken..." so that "...opera is not, as some have claimed a corrupted theatre – theatre is impoverished opera."

'Nuff said!   – Gerry Brody, "Opera's Regular Guy"

*Oxford University Press, New York, 1978

PRELUDE

OPERA: YOU NEVER KNEW YOU LOVED IT! is decidedly not "yet another opera book"!

It is offered as a primer for people of all ages who have been reluctant, for similar reasons, to open the door to a unique aural and visual experience. The needlessly elusive dish that is *opera* is presented here as a palatable appetizer which should much enhance the cuisine to follow. Recommendations for more sumptuous dining are given in the final section. The purpose of this approach is to tempt a larger customer base into trying a wonderfully nutritious product which can also taste great if introduced in a comprehensible and timely manner. I will not call "spaghetti with tomato sauce" *capelli d'angelo pomodoro** to pander to an elite *gourmetism* and simultaneously obtaining a far higher price on a much fancier menu. This tendency, I most strongly feel, has served to separate *opera* from the folks who do not *yet* realize that they can come to love the all encompassing vocal art form. The title of this effort derives from a rating sheet comment of one of my students**: "Opera: I never knew I loved it until I took this course with Brody."

Some, including a few I regard as friends, have occasionally described me as "an elitist in reverse," a brand I have worn with some discomfort. Over time, though, I have come to much prefer another appellation, one which should conjure the proud swagger of a comic-book – nay! a noble operatic – *caped hero*: and now (scored for multiple trumpets), enter **"The Antidote"**!

*Italian for "angel hair with tomato sauce" but still good ole "spaghetti".
**Average age 71. I have conducted courses in Opera Appreciation as part of the life-long-learning Elderhostel program for many years.

RECITATIVE

"GOOD AFTERNOON, WFCF OPERA LOVERS, CURRENT AND FUTURE."

Immediately after turning on my microphone a dozen years ago on my very first *The Joy of Opera* radio program, I experienced a moment of panic in the realization that there were live humans out there actually listening to what I was about to say. A quick inhaling gulp and, *mirabile dictu**, out came those totally spontaneous words. I could not have chosen a better and more appropriate opening if I thought it through for weeks. These words have now preceded over 600 broadcasts. It was *because* of that initial dread that the improvised words were born. They summed up all I have always believed about *opera*– that if two obstacles and an illusory hurdle could be overcome, a vast virgin vein of new opera lovers could be tapped. The primary purpose of this work is to facilitate that barrier removal and subsequent excavation, an effort quite realistically achievable, as a thick bundle of comments I have received (several from former opera *haters*) so attest. At its best, *opera* is the most potent and moving of art forms, but it must be fed carefully. "Mangia Bene!"**

The autobiographical references are in no way narcissistic: I am much too old, and professionally comfortable, for such indulgence. Specifically purposeful, these *folksy tidbits* intertwine with the historical, instructional and recommendation sections and are primarily shared to explain, in some measure, the development of my personal *approach*, so often noted by my listeners and senior students. Honestly, however, I never had that proverbial *clue* as to just what this *approach* constitutes. Some things, probably relating to impulsive passion, do best when they are simply left unanalyzed.

*"Wonderful to say"
**"Eat well"

For me, it was a *voice* that did it (Chapter 2). For you, it was or may be an *aria*, an ensemble, a single chord or even a dramatic pause– *opera* has a good few– which should never be confused with mere silence. At any rate, the choice of the addictive agent is strictly yours.

My intent, simply focused, is to increase the number of you, in exclaiming, with some sense of surprise:

"Opera: I Never Knew I Loved It!"

Part I

"A Stentorian New World"

Opera: (That Hodge-Podge of the late Renaissance)
Stentor: (A Greek Herald noted for a loud voice)

1 - The Word, The Wealth and The Wall

> *"Render the needlessly complex simple–*
> *Make not the simple complex–*
> *In this fertile soil, learning will flourish."*
>   *–Opera's Regular Guy*

Opera means *work* or *works*, the Italian singular or plural–depending on the chosen dictionary definition– of the Latin *opus*. How was it that this odd word came to define a bold new vocal art form in the last few years of the 16th century? A probable explanation concerns an English chronicler who was in Florence compiling data on the state of the arts in Italy. Regarding the nascent vocal experiment, the founding Italians referred to their collaborative effort as *l'opera nostra* (our work) or *l'opera musica* (musical work). Curiously, the Englishman employed the word *opera* to define the art form itself though the Italians never so described it: their choices were *favola per musica* (musical fable), *dramma per musica* (musical drama) or *melodramma* (then also meaning music drama). It would, however, only be *opera* that would hold and, as we will see, perhaps no better term could have inadvertently been used since, through the fortuitous misinterpretation, the literary Englishman was indeed describing *the works*. The nobly born founders of *opera* were amateur poets and musicians seeking a *higher form* and a backer. Higher than what? Other than as employees of the church or the court, performing musicians were widely regarded as little more than street entertainers, urchins, and rogues. The small group of vocal visionaries sought to rededicate and reglorify the classic Greek drama by adding background sets to song in a merging of all the arts: poetry, painting and music. This ambitious effort came late in that magnificent creative explosion, born in Italy in the 14th century, known as the *Renaissance*, so wonderfully building a glorious bridge between the Middle Ages and modernity in Europe. It is of interest that among the founding group was one Vincenzo Galilei who wrote extensively and critically on the musical theory of the day and would exert influence on the first *chefs d'l'opera in musica**. Of greater cosmic scope was the fact that this intellect fathered the astronomer Galileo.

Thus, as that brilliant beacon began to flicker and fade as the 16th century squeezed out its final few years, the stage was being set for an innovative last gasp – this platform was the *opera* stage and it became immediately apparent that adorning this setting required those *inseparable siblings*: money and prestige. This would not change in the next 400 years.

A particularly supportive benefactor appeared in the person of the Florentine nobleman Count Giovanni Bardi. His court became a most welcoming second home for the passionate group of poets, artists and composers known as the *camerata* (the chamber). The Count served in much the same manner as a *proud as a peacock* father of highly studious offspring. The *chemicals* of the *great experiment* were tested for almost two decades in the Count's inner sanctum until *eurekas* were heard just before the new century was born.

The founders were ever juggling the several balls that were formative opera, into the air with varying degrees of success. Which art, if any, would dominate? What was the correct formula for the proper glorification of the pure Greek drama? The original composers were passionate amateurs not sufficiently equipped for such a scope. Fate would not keep us waiting too long in delivering Claudio Monteverdi (1567-1643), a professional genius once in the employ of the authentic Duke of Mantua**, who made the *toddler* not only respectable but gloriously so. For the sake of consistent reference, *opera* saw the light of day in the year 1600 as Europe entered the modern age of art and science. This coincided exactly with the origin of mechanical stagecraft, also springing from Italian soil.

*"Chiefs of musical works"
**In Verdi's *Rigoletto*, the Mantua lineage was resurrected in the personage of the libertine Duke when the Austrian censors refused to allow the French King Francis I to be portrayed.

The ingredients were all there to be joined and melded under white heat: the neoclassical poetry, the luminescent frescoes and canvases, the beginning of song outside of the church and the *original* stage gimmicks. It couldn't miss and surely didn't.

We can so vividly relate to what happened next. As soon as it was clear that the new art was marketable, the race for supremacy in extravaganza was on. Which noble court would become *au currant* with the most lavish? It spread through Italy and much of Europe with the speed of an epidemic and, from the start, the matter of which *box* would best reflect the noblest of nobles, the fairest of them all was of paramount importance. This, too, would remain constant for the ensuing four centuries.

The first public opera house opened in Venice about 40 years after *opera* emerged from the womb of the Florentine court and the action was all north of Rome at this point. The early impresari immediately realized that their baby could rake in major profits from a desirous widening audience. "He who pays the piper calls the tune" could have been an early aria in this rapidly expanding venue. *Public opera*, however, is a misleading term as it was immediately realized that it could only survive with noble backing as well. Coastal Venice was a wealthy place and theaters appeared almost spontaneously. What should sound quite familiar to us was that *big bucks* were spent on star singers and elaborate mechanized sets while the remainder of most opera houses were quite meager. Comedy would soon enter the new art form, frequently spoofing its stiffly serious prim and proper relatives.

Let's end this initial chapter with a snapshot of the new art form as it would ultimately evolve. Gradually, but inexorably, vocal music ventured out of the church and its *polyphonic** form in the late Renaissance. Church *mystery plays* were probably the earliest detectable ancestors of *opera*. The new Italian art form sprang from *experiments* by a group of aristocratic individuals with the *laboratory* lovingly provided by a wealthy Florentine Count. It spread like wildfire, first through northern Italy and then through virtually all of courtly Europe.

*"Many voices"

Boldly, *opera* proceeded to showcase Greek gods and demi-gods, then Roman humans (but super heroic humans to be sure) and then the kings, queens, and court royalty not materially different from the venue of the birth of the art form itself. Very haltingly, however, did the *regular guy* and *gal* appear on the opera stage as leads and it would take a quarter millennium for that to be accepted. Within the courtly background of *La Traviata* (1853) the great Verdi *hinted* at it in the poignant character of Violetta Valery, and the Frenchman Bizet hit us between the eyes with the gypsy *Carmen* in 1875. (It is not surprising, in retrospect, that both works initially failed.) Finally, by the last decade of the 19th century *we* were in big time with all our facets, not the least of which were treachery, jealously, infidelity, vengeance, and the penchant for violence: in other words, the *food* on which *opera* thrives. The main difference between us and the royals is that we made little attempt to obscure our behavior. By the turn of the 20th century, the bold truth (*verismo*) was undeniable – we were *opera* and *opera* was *us*!

This brings us, in conclusion, to another form of *verismo*: NO MONEY, NO OPERA! The most expensive of all the arts, *opera* cannot survive without its modern court and this has been changeless since the inception. This court, palpably discernable, presides over the Metropolitan Opera Association in New York City or Tinytown USA, where a new opera company is established for cultural enrichment and its attendant status-flaunting. It is the strenuous and tenuous relationship between the art and its food supply. Styles may change, but this fragile balancing act between the *royal* and the *soil*, the prince and the peasant, is ever present. Between the two, a **wall** has always existed and, as with all such barriers, it serves to keep *out* or keep *in*.

A quote from the book *Caruso* by Howard Greenfield* is particularly illustrative. Discussing the Metropolitan Opera's opening night on November 23, 1903, Mr. Greenfield focuses on the recent alterations to the then 20-year-old theater, including the gilding of boxes, the enlargement of the stage, and the lowering of

*Da Capo Press, 1983, New York

the pit. He goes on to tell that "...only the glamorous audience, with its plethora of Astors, Vanderbilts, Belmonts, Blisses, Roosevelts, and Morgans, remained unchanged from that which habitually attended the seasons opening: it was an audience notoriously more interested in fashion and jewels than in whatever might be happening on stage." It surely didn't matter that what was *happening on stage* that evening was the American debut of Enrico Caruso.

The purpose of this book, and emphasized throughout , is to invite in some *regular folk* who have regarded the *wall* (as does your author) as artificial, arrogantly ostentatious, forbidding and, in the final analysis, meaningless. The invitation, therefore, will be far more readily accepted if it is sent *before* the *wall* is encountered.

2 - The Bug

I had the wonderful good fortune of being born into a musical family where the genes, traceable to Eastern Europe a century and a half ago, ran through my mother's side. Paternally, the ancestral name was not among the millions truncated by impatient bureaucrats on Ellis Island; it referred to the town *Brody*, once part of Poland but currently in northwest Ukraine. Of personal interest, several people have related that the village was particularly noted as a cultural hub for music, poetry and art, the very ingredients, come to think of it, which created *opera* itself. The family's *mystery man* (most families tend to have at least one) is my maternal grandfather who was rarely spoken of even by people who spoke of everyone else. When his name did come up, it was always in the context of being a *fine violinist*. Sure enough, a recently uncovered photograph taken in a New York City studio around 1900 shows him *fiddle in hand*. My mother, a proficient pianist, possessed a clear and accurate *leggiera** voice which my friends loved to hear, frequently requesting that I accompany her. My children are particularly musical, two professionally, and we continue to expect a truly prodigious issue as the grandchildren continue to proliferate in all directions. My first vague memories relate to playing the gargantuan Horace Waters upright piano while composing music. The family has always maintained that I played remarkably well at two and one-half with both hands. I vividly recall being adulated by grownups at age four and not understanding why since I thought *everybody* could do that; it took years for me to realize otherwise, that people had different gifts and abilities- thank goodness! All this is intended as personal perspective and quite sufficient for our purposes here.

---

*Light– this type of soprano is often, and inaccurately, called a *coloratura* which is a florid technique that once had to be mastered by *all* singers, male and female.

When World War II ended, records were short-play shellac discs whirling at 78 RPM. The 33⅓ vinyl long-play format would be introduced three years later by Columbia which would now grace us with a state of relaxation that was imaginable only in our dreams. The main solo instruments (piano and violin) were difficult to record on early acoustic 78s as were the supporting orchestras. They were totally eclipsed in home popularity by the operatic voice where an aria or duet would neatly fit on one side of a 12-inch disc, allowing some four and one-half minutes of listening. These records were expensive and money was hard to come by, yet many homes of the time had at least a few Caruso's, Galli-Curci's and McCormack's and ours was one of them. There was always music and my preference gradually leaned to the tenor voice. When a very early RCA Victor complete opera (the 1950 *Rigoletto**) on the LP format was played, I took a particular liking to the American tenor Jan Peerce. Over time, Peerce's recordings were purchased on all three formats (78, 45 and 33⅓). The latter now allowed us to sit down, actually relax, and keep the record playing for over 20 minutes with a diamond needle that lasted a year, not quite *permanent* as Columbia originally termed it, but a major leap forward to be sure.

Many of my Brooklyn friends in the early 1950s were first generation Italian-Americans. This coincided with the meteoric ascent of the short-lived Mario Lanza, a naturally gifted but musically undisciplined singer who met his highly successful destiny in Hollywood. While Lanza never performed in stage opera, a few of his finest recordings were viscerally thrilling and rivaled the great tenors. A strange *war* began between Frank Fontana and me as to who was better, Peerce (Jacob Pincus Perelmuth of New York City) or Lanza (Alfred Arnold Cocozza of Philadelphia)? The battles were joined when we would play, one after another, the same song or aria by both tenors. The level of intensity would frequently rise alarmingly but it became clear that no victories nor surrenders would ever be forthcoming.

*The first complete opera released by RCA Victor on the LP format. Columbia achieved this two years earlier which was fitting since it innovated the concept.

Some time passed when another of my Italian friends, Frank Costignaro, hereinafter known as *Frankie*, entered the fray in saying that his opera loving grandmother said that "...some Swedish guy" is the best of all. "What's the name of this Swedish guy?" "Juicy Jurling"! Little did I know that this hilarious mispronunciation immediately preceded the first defining moment of my opera-loving life as Frankie left, saying he would ask if he could bring a record back. In a few minutes, he returned with one 12-inch 78 (in its original brown paper jacket) RCA Red Seal disc. On one side "Che Gelida Manina" from *La Bohème* and on the other "Celeste Aida" from *Aida*. Ah! The tenor's name was Jussi Bjöerling*. The *Bohème* aria went on first: Rodolfo's *racconto*** was previously part of the Peerce-Lanza battlefield. The scratchy disc began with the six measures of orchestral introduction, the pause and "Che Gelida Manina, Se La Lasci Riscaldar" (what a cold little hand, allow me to warm it). I was instantly *riveted* to the intrinsic sound of that voice, pure, youthful and innocent but, above all, uniquely beautiful and produced with an indescribable ease. Though pristine as Alpine air, *that voice* also hinted, just *hinted*, of a vague longing; the simultaneous combination was sheer *melodic magic* and not quite of this world. All at once, the Peerce-Lanza crusades were rendered both spurious and adolescent. But adolescents we were, desperately trying to hold on to these last innocent years as we felt a change coming and, somehow, knowing that it would never again be the same. It would be a mere *blink of an eye* to the unthinkable, the exiting of the Brooklyn Dodgers to Los Angeles in 1957. And just a few more *blinks* from that loss to the advent of international terrorism a generation or so later, when we could not then conceive of *anything* more traumatic than our beloved *Bums* abandoning us so callously.

*The early RCA Victor recordings listed an 'e' as the fourth letter of the tenor's surname. Only later did the family inform that the correct spelling was Björling.
**Account- this term is often used to describe this aria.

And I would never again be the same as that mesmerizing sound *peaked* and *valleyed* with an exquisite ease as the poet continued telling the frail young woman that although he lives in squalor, his soul is a millionaire who builds castles in the sky. That voice now leapt to the high C on the word "*speranza*" (hope) as it asked for the response in a whispering "*vi piaccia dir*" (please tell me) of haunting softness. The *aria* took exactly four minutes and thirty seconds but it still remains vivid and frozen in time. I have no recollection whatever as to whether the *flip side** was ever played then and it didn't matter. The *bug* had *bitten* and I was instantly addicted. Of far greater importance, owing solely to the sound of this voice, I now longed to dig deeper into what was going on, what do the words mean, why, where and how? "If this be *opera*, sing on" Shakespeare may have exclaimed if he had heard Björling. After all, the infant *opera* was just born southeastward when the great bard flourished but it was not yet taken seriously in his native England. He surely would have loved it though and, so fittingly, his plays were chosen to furnish *libretti* for his long adoring disciple Giuseppe Verdi for use in the two greatest masterworks of Italian opera, *Otello* and *Falstaff*.

Over a half century has passed now and it is time to formally say thanks to my parents for the musical genetics, the huge piano, the records and the loving support. Thanks Frank, for those wonderful *battles* where nobody was ever seriously wounded. But above all here, a profound *grazie* to Frankie's opera loving *nanna* for allowing him to bring the sound of that *Swedish guy's* voice into my home and into my soul.

Doubtless, I would have met the splendid tenor rather soon in a different venue but the *gestalt* of that *epiphany* was uniquely special and will never fade from my mind.

And, thanks for *The Joy of Opera* where I have done to others what the Björling record did to me!

*A now obsolete term since CDs are not *flipped*.

3 - The Collecting

I guess I'll simply plead no contest and proudly wear the label that psychiatrists term *obsessive-compulsive disorder* as my *stentorian new world* now only knew immediate gratification. And, as with all such addictions, I found that I needed more to remain the same.

The collecting began only with records but soon grew to covet origins, language, and overall history, all things operatic, as much as I could absorb and I sought to absorb all. First and always foremost, however, were the records. The *reverses* of 12-inch LPs were often *vest pocket* encyclopedias. How I loved, and love, those disks when, with only occasional applications of cellophane tape, their jackets would last forever. Contrast this with our high-tech 21st century CD cases which crack at a cruel glance, liner notes soon ripped to shreds and the plastic holding tabs breaking off at the initial opening.

My *octopus* was born small but, gradually, the strengthened tentacles acquired in several directions simultaneously: a Mozart concerto here, another Björling, Caruso, or Gigli, then the sopranos, and the lower voices, the complete operas, the complete symphonies, Beethoven, Brahms, Tchaikovsky, then back to opera with a touted *next Caruso* (who wasn't) and a *can't miss phenom* (who missed). At the peak of my frenzied quest, I probably embraced over 6,000 records. Memory, and honesty, are vague here but all my precious platters were played once, many several times over time and my special sweethearts were worn thin and worn out. Then, there were those impulsive magic moments when a long forgotten entity was specifically chosen and anointed with the rarified privilege of again adorning a turntable.

Never, however, has my musical acquisition addiction been more exposed as a problem than when I changed residences much too frequently. There is simply no romanticizing this– transporting those records truly rivaled the travails of Atlas. Precious though they were, my gems were ponderously heavy treasure.

After one move, I noticed that the back tires on my car were bowing out, like a novice ice skater unable to stand vertically, necessitating a most expensive replacement of springs and straightening of axle. Clearly, the burdens of my sonic hoarding affliction could no longer be ignored. An elemental choice now loomed: shedding at least *some* of my recordings and/or staying put in one place for a reasonable length of time. There were also some socially responsible options such as yard sales and flea markets so I could convince myself of the sensibility of musical *recycling*, but no eminently logical approach would ever see the light of day.

Finally, to the old quaint City of St. Augustine* came my wife (Susan) and myself, with a scant few necessities and the 6,000 long playing records in what appeared to be an endless line of heavy duty corrugated wine cartons. These sturdy containers measured just a bit over 12" x 12" (inside measurement) rendering them ideal for transporting record albums. Though logic would dictate that they were manufactured to hold and protect glass wine bottles, I invoked the *theory of dual use* by which they were equally designed so that I could get my *family* safely to Florida. Though the printed labels said Gallo, Fetzer, and Masson, to me they clearly read VERDI, WAGNER AND BIZET.

The *crème de le crème* were the boxed albums of complete operas, usually two to four LPs with notes and side-by-side *libretto* (little book) translations from the original language to English. I now had it all: a tolerant wife, our early retirement oasis, and my 6,000 offspring. Rarely was I ever reminded of the omni-presence of that collection, even though a lingering sense of guilt pervaded. It was now, however, only vocal and opera music to which I seemed to pay attention.

*Founded by the Spanish in 1565, St. Augustine, FL (40 miles south of Jacksonville) is the oldest continuously occupied settlement in what is now the United States. I was taught that the Jamestown English were the first Europeans here in 1607. What else were we told that is simply not supported by the facts?

Though Susan, at this point, took only a good few deep breaths, I knew the sacrifice she made– there were those boxes lining every closet, filling every nook and cranny and coming perilously close to invading our bedroom.

I bit a *bomb of a bullet* and discarded every non-operatic/vocal LP record. Incredibly, it felt greatly liberating and when it was done, I was reduced to a sacrosanct 3,000. Only when we visited our children in the North did I occasionally gravitate to the Princeton Record Exchange and revert to a *dollar a disk fix*. And, though she never uttered it, I well knew what my wife would think: the two questions which have plagued neurotic record collectors for eons were now midway between her consciousness and her lips. And *this* when I just did something *unthinkable*, unloading half of my collection! Surely, that had to count for *something*!!

The setting was July, 1993. Among my treasured 3,000 lay a certain 12" long playing record: destiny would soon focus her sights on this album in a most wonderful way, and *just* before Susan found the perfect spring-board from which to comfortably ask the dreaded duet of questions which were decidedly *not* "...to be or not to be?" Those were for another dilemma in another time and place.

4 - "Call for Igor Gorin"

Yes, indeed, to little old St. Augustine we had come with a little car, a little furniture, two extremely unhappy little cats and that mammoth lot of *misprinted* record cartons. Very slowly and methodically did I open them and, yet again, vertically arrange those platters according to my long held and rigidly compulsive system: alphabetical by category and sub-category, left to right– tenors, baritones, basses, and then the same with the females– sopranos, mezzo-sopranos and contraltos (see Glossary for definitions). It was still mandatory that I know just where each was in the increasingly remote event that it would ever become realistically pertinent in this modern age of the tiny digital compact disc. Yet, exactly such an occurrence would soon present itself in a fashion that would test even the credulity of a Hollywood scriptwriter.

When we set up house in the old Spanish inspired city, classical music was broadcast via Jacksonville Public Radio (subsequently replaced by a talk format). During a request fund raiser just a few months after our arrival, a call came in from a woman in nearby Palm Coast asking for the baritone Igor Gorin. Ukrainian by birth, Gorin had a particularly rich and resonant voice with an effortless top register which could ascend to the tenor range. The singer was often heard on such wonderful early live TV programs as *The Voice of Firestone* (with conductor Howard Barlow) and *The Bell Telephone Hour* (where Donald Vorhees directed the orchestra). Gorin was also on the Met's roster for a brief period. Now, however, the fine artist was virtually obscure. The program's host possessed no studio recordings and broadcasted an appeal to the listening audience for a long-playing record or CD "...if one exists..." My "I have it" was followed by an expression on Susan's face which can only translate to a disbelieving "aaaah, c'mon!"

And, since I had just again meticulously arranged my dormant offspring, I knew not only that he *existed* but exactly where he was reposing. I went upstairs, nudged him gently, softly blew the dust off and rekindled my affection after so many years.

There, in pristine condition on the long defunct Urania label, was *Igor Gorin Sings Great Baritone Arias* with Vorhees conducting. Almost immediately, after informing an incredulous Susan that I found it, she began (and I immediately felt it coming) to *finally* ask those two questions to which there are no logical answers, the questions no record-collecting fanatic ever wants to hear. But now she had her worthy stage, a radio request which the station could not fulfill but which I *could* and the attendant on-air appeal which had to be personally aimed directly at ME. With a most loving smile did the words emanate:

> *"Darling, when was the last time you played that record?"*
> and...
> *"Dearest, what are you going to do with all those records?"*

"You don't understand!" is the only possible response. How could she understand when I couldn't? One thing, however, is crystal clear: these questions have always been designed to spur the most active response possible of getting rid of *old baggage*, in this case *old records*. And, after her eminently logical queries coupled with the latent guilt over my collection, I actually picked up the receiver, called the studio and informed the grateful host that I, indeed, had the coveted Gorin artifact on the LP format adding that I would (I never said "gladly") donate it for airing so the lady's request could be accommodated. Profuse on-air "...thank you's" followed. The very next day, we drove the northward 40 miles to the radio station. The touch of resentment I initially felt toward Susan for "making me do this" was quickly mitigated by the undeniable fact that, at no time, did she even approximate holding that *gun* to my head. No! I did it, did it alone and must bear the entire responsibility. The radio host gave us the warmest sentiments of gratitude and informed us that he personally met Gorin many years ago in conjunction with some vocal study. A fascinating personal tour of the studio followed– all those LP's and CD's, that wonderful equipment and that stately microphone.

For perhaps the first time in my adult life, I felt envy for another human being. What a fortunate man he was to be able to play opera recordings for a living and then discuss them with his listeners, truly a state of nirvana. There was no getting around it, I was envious. How could I have ever known, in these moments, that harboring this foreign emotion would be of the shortest possible duration, but I'm just a trifle ahead of myself.

A subtle, but lingering, sense of guilt pervaded as I gradually returned to the real world during the drive back. I knew exactly what was causing it– why did I not donate the cassette copy instead of the original LP? This question has never left me in comfort because, to this day, I feel like I gave a *child* away, one of only 3,000 now to be sure, but of my precious lineage nonetheless.

Many times since have I come very close to calling the station to ask for my *baby's* return in exchange for its *cloned cassette*, but I never did. Could it have been a necessary *sacrifice* for all the recent good fortune in my life? At any rate, time dulled, but never completely healed, that guilty ache of cutting Igor Gorin loose. What has that baritone ever done except produce those wonderful rich sounds? Incredibly, however, this would not be the end of the matter for an astounding *coincidence* would present itself a few months later which would form the foundation for Part III of this effort.

Before that, however, there is Part II, without which I would never have had the pleasure of hearing so many of you exclaim that you have come to truly love a uniquely comprehensive vocal art form because of ME! And, in case you may have temporarily forgotten, that art form was, rather oddly, called *opera*!

Part II

"The
Obstacles"

and

"The Antidotes"

5 - The Ignorant, The Arrogant and The Sycophant

> *You Are What You Pretend To Be–*
> *So Be Careful What You Pretend To Be!*
> *–Kurt Vonnegut*

As *opera* approached the middle of its second century, a critical fork in the road was encountered. Simultaneously, and providentially, a composer came of age who possessed a properly calibrated compass. Christoph Willibald Gluck (1714-1787), midway between Handel and Mozart, successfully, and mercifully, rescued opera from its singers. Called *The Great Reformer*, Gluck redirected opera to its original concept– paying reverent vocal homage to Greco-Roman stage drama– and *applied the brakes* on the wildly adulated *castrati** (surgically induced male sopranos) from going beyond interpretive license to altering the composer's music at will. Why was this practice ever allowed in the first place? $$$$$! The immense popularity of these unique eunuchs cannot be overstated and their appearances made very rich men of impresari and composers– most notably Handel– whose bulging bankrolls totally quelled artistic outrage. Gluck's integrity and universal respect facilitated a realigning of the operatic track and, in so doing (though he couldn't know it), he also laid a solid roadbed for the just born Mozart (1756-1791) and the stage would be set for that wondrous genius of the 18th century to so gloriously *pave the road* for the 19th.

Though not dealing with quite so vital a matter as saving the art form from its *coloraturistic songbirds*, my delicate challenge concerns insulating and protecting *opera* from the *opera goer*. This territory requires traversing white-water rapids and is quite generally steered away from in more traditional publications dealing with the subject. The highly sensitive area, however, represents

---

*I highly recommend a 1994 Italian-French film (Sony) *Farinelli* (1705-1782), a beautiful and accurate account of the most legendary of all the *castrati*. These phenomenal singers combined the sound of females with the power of males.

one of the two major obstacles to a wider popular following for *opera* and, consequently, must not be ignored.

First, and foremost, it is absolutely vital at the outset that I clarify what is meant by the term *opera goer* in this context. Clearly, it does not at all refer to the ticket-buying patron who attends a performance for the purpose of deriving some degree of *emotional massage* from the sensually powerful vocal and visual experience. Contrarily, it specifically pertains to the individual who takes up a plush seat for reasons not even remotely connected to "...whatever might be happening on stage."*

The basic dilemma is that the bulk of these *'goers* also provides the life fluid without which the great art petrifies– that precious infusion is called MONEY. With enough money, great good can even spring from greatest *chutzpah*.

Consider the following excerpt from the memoirs of the legendary soprano Lilli Lehmann regarding an incident occurring at the *then* premier New York City opera house, the Academy of Music, in its 1879-80 season:

> "As, on a particular evening, one of the millionairesses did not receive the box in which she intended to shine because another woman had anticipated her, the husband of the former took prompt action and caused the Metropolitan Opera House to rise."**

The surname of the *former* was Vanderbilt. It should also not be forgotten that the still earlier Astor Place Opera House perished for the very same reason, insufficient stations to allow the newly crowned American *royals* to *glisten*.

*Op. Cit., Chapter 1
**John Briggs, *Requiem for a Yellow Brick Brewery*, Little, Brown and Company, Boston, 1969

From the very start, then, the spotlights simultaneously focused on *two* operas, one on the composer's stage and the other in the ornately gilded box. As it was in the last years of the 16th century, and as it will likely ever be, this marriage of convenience is a bittersweet relationship of absolute necessity. Why, then, my attempt to distinguish *opera* from its IV solution, without which the patient immediately withers on the vocal vine?

Prior to beginning any of the several courses I teach, under the surreptitious agenda of *Opera: You Never Knew You Loved It*, I always ask for a show of hands response to four questions, initially asked within the context of general curiosity. Gradually, this evolved into a gauge of how the thrust of my course should be directed in terms of specific levels of simplicity or complexity and, over time, the technique essentially took on the more formalized structure of a research study to confirm, or refute, my long held hypothesis that two formidable obstacles and one perceived hurdle repellently serve to turn away potential guests at the door of the operatic inn.

The questions are these:
1. "How many of you truly know/love *opera*?"
2. "How many enjoy classical music **including** *opera*?"
3. "How many enjoy classical music **except** for *opera*?"
4. "How many truly hate and despise *opera*?"
   (I implore total honesty here.)

The bell curve has proven remarkably consistent: a scant few hands raised to questions 1 and 4 and the great bulk fairly well split between questions 2 and 3. Occasionally, a high response to question 4 occurs at which point I immediately play the last part of the pivotal 1936 Björling *Bohème aria* after I offer a brief *stage setting* explanation. This continues to serve as a *salve* on an *open wound* to those who viscerally cringe at the sound of the voice operatic.

Of particular interest to me were the responses to questions 3 and 4.

Why, curiously, was *opera* negatively separated from instrumental music by so many intelligent senior citizens of flexible open mind and why, though fairly rare, the extreme level of vitriol regarding the wonderful vocal art? Honest discussion and analysis had clearly provided the answers: *Opera* is too regularly associated with haughtiness, artificiality and social gamesmanship and, even worse, has forced an assault on the ears accompanying their youthful possessor to an improper first exposure with singers whose vocal organs did not at all fall gently on those formative auditory appendages. The result of such duality can be catastrophic for a lifetime and is further detailed in the next chapter as well.

The courses I teach (*Opera Appreciation* they should be called) have consistently converted folks, despite themselves, for reasons most relevant here since they pinpoint the basic purpose of this effort, that the barriers to *opera* can be far more easily surmounted if *the bug* bites first, if *opera* (the vocal art form) *embraces* before the *goer* and the *blower effaces*. The bite of this bug is to be courted, not feared, as it can provide a permanent immunity against the adverse side effects of the *operatic sideshow* where it also serves to distance that *puppetry* to its proper place backstage and the further back the better.

When sifting to get at that proverbial *nitty-gritty*, as is now the case, literal definitions serve best:

A IGNORANT – lack of knowledge, unaware
B ARROGANT – exaggerating one's importance in an
   overbearing, presumptuous or superior manner and,
C SYCOPHANT – a self-serving flatterer.

It is of the most vital importance that young minds, ears and eyes A be properly exposed to opera before B and C cast their discouraging shadows. Consequently, great caution should be exercised to protect against that pervasive entity the "Igarrophant" (please refer to the Glossary), a creature which has proven to be particularly resistant to the traditional methods of pest control.

Many an account, by young and old alike, has been related to me as to why *opera–* and specifically *opera–* has been elusive and awkward to embrace. Though the settings may have differed, the core theme is constant and undeniable: too many folks feel downright uncomfortable in, and around, *opera* and, sadly but truthfully– with darn good reason– the *ambiance* has, yet again, ruined what could have been a delicious and nutritious dining experience.

A vibrant personal memory comes to mind at this juncture. In the late 1950's, when the Metropolitan Opera allowed audience entry after an act started, two ladies filed in and sat directly in front of me during a performance of *Tosca*. As a result of their latecoming, they failed to read the insertion in the program informing that the indisposed lead tenor Mario del Monaco was replaced, at very short notice, by a stand-in (memory recalls either Barry Morrell or Daniele Barioni) who began very tentatively and struggled quite badly through "Recondita Armonia,"* coming early in Act One. One of the couldn't be silent *tardies* proclaimed quite loudly that del Monaco was "...in superb voice tonight," followed by a stifled "...oooooh" when I leaned forward and meekly informed her of the last minute casting change. What occurred there was the uninvited, unfortunate and entirely unnecessary covering of *ignorance* with *arrogance*.

While the general such scenario takes various guises and venues, by far the most common may be termed *cocktail party opera* where the vocal art form is **talked** rather than **felt** and where the score is distinctly annotated as follows:

> ♪ **Recitative** (con dolcezza - sweetly) "Were you at the *opera* last evening?"
> ♪ **Aria** (con brio - with verve) "O*f course* darling, wasn't it WON-der-ful!"**
> ♪ **Ballet** - "The Dance of the Sycophants"

And, as with that pink drummer rabbit powered by that inexhaustible battery, this beat indeed goes *on* and, endlessly, *on*.

*"Contrasting Harmonies"
**In my experience, the sole purpose of the goer's *going* is the very event of the *being there*.

In conclusion, let's summarize and graphically illuminate the stage action at this point. As the splendid, blended vocal art form compassionately looks down from Mt. Olympus at pure theater as "...impoverished opera," modern incarnations mimic that *queen of opera goers* who, in her haughty hubris, would ironically fertilize the embryo of the Metropolitan Opera House in late 19th century New York City where, with minimal complications, that huge offspring would be born only three scant years later. Between these most disparate mileposts lies the richest of fertile fields, the soil of which can nourish a large group of devoted disciples to the 400-year-old *experiment* which, as though through wizardry, forged *all* arts into one magical amalgam. Too easily, however, can this land be rendered fallow by unnecessary and unrelated contaminants. This small book sings to the former. Let's hear it now...loud and clear! Three operatic cheers for the melodic naturopath!

6 - Preventing Child Abuse

In this work's final portion, specific suggestions are offered for a benign method of dipping the young into the operatic baptism pool. Also addressed there is the far more daunting matter of reversing damage already done when the tenuous initiation procedure was ignored or traumatically accomplished. Indeed, the single strongest repellent to any eventual appreciation of *opera* is an aural frontal assault on the uninitiated novice. Though a formidable challenge, the prognosis need not be bleak as I, with gleeful satisfaction, have personally realized with regularity. Accordingly, the following pair of long past illustrative incidents could have had a very different outcome had a flickering sign been heeded:

WARNING!
YOU'RE ENTERING THE UNIQUE REALM OF OPERA:
PROCEED WITH CAUTION!

This first fascinating piece of family folklore was related a few years ago by one of my senior students and it is profound in its utter simplicity. An otherwise intellectual octogenarian, the family patriarch had never attended a live opera and, wishing to expand his universe in his golden years, the children systematically and successfully broke down any protesting defenses. During the fateful few hours– nobody recalled the opera or the singers– he didn't utter a solitary word of complaint or grimace of pain. When it was finally over, he was gently asked how he liked it. "Oh, it wasn't *too* bad, but did they have to sing so *loud*?"

A far more dramatic account comes from the memory bank of a most delightful member of the *Brody's Roadies Club** for *opera addicts*, many recently *hooked*.

---

*This term was applied by a student in the Elderhostel program referring to a group of seniors who followed me around from course to course at different locations.

This riveting incident, a veritable worst case scenario, resoundingly underscores that introducing *opera* to the young is a delicate area near which peril always lurks. The husband (now deceased) of my *Roadie* grew up in New York City where his parents had a subscription to the old Metropolitan Opera House on 39th Street and Broadway. Some time in the late 1930's, he was taken to see *Siegfried*, (the third, most opaque and least melodic of Wagner's mammoth tetralogy *The Ring of the Nibelung*). This, his baby step into the immense world of *live opera*, unfortunately coincided with the specific series his parents possessed. The chronology also renders it quite likely that the title role that evening may have been sung by the legendary *Heldentenor* (heroic) Lauritz Melchior. Of this, however, he had no memory as repression and amnesia set in quickly. It, and all else related to that experience, was forever emblazoned in horror on his adolescent psyche and the very *thought* of *opera* became an anathema ever since. His wife related that after one or two failed *seduction* attempts, the hope of his ever accompanying her was forever abandoned. She wistfully wondered how he would have responded to my approach but, since the announced listings included the very word *opera*, that reality would never have come to pass no matter how long he may have lived.

There is a quasi-cosmic link between the two gentlemen as the innocent question of the former is sonorously answered by the latter: "Yes, my kindred, in *Siegfried* they most assuredly *did* have to sing so loudly."

The importance of these accounts cannot be overstated. Young and old alike have regularly struggled to explain to me why they either simply do not like, or downright abhor, opera. The previous chapter dealt with one reason and now we arrive at the second, and more potent, the intrinsic sound of the operatic voice itself which, at its least comfortable, can be a viscerally painful experience.

Why did both these formative (even though one was over 80 at the time) males react as they did? Allow me to pose an explanation. The opera voice does not naturally embrace the auditory sense of the uninitiated. The training of budding opera singers has always been a mysterious and highly inexact science.

By contrast, consider the teaching of gifted piano and violin students as cases in point. There is no such thing as a professional pianist or violinist who has not mastered, step by disciplined step, the fundamentals of fingering or bowing. Sight reading is a *sine qua non** (couldn't resist that phrase) for any hope of a career. Gifted piano and violin teachers have produced front ranked virtuosi with regularity. For example, lineage can be traced from Van Cliburn– through his teacher Lhevinne and downwards in time– to instructors who studied with Beethoven, who was a pupil of Haydn, and so on and so forth to the very beginnings of the progressive percussive keyboard itself. Likewise, from Jascha Heifetz through Auer to Joseph Joachim (Brahms' favorite violinist) and down through time. Similarly, as with the acting profession, many offspring of famous pianists and violinists frequently follow with full careers of their own as much has been taught and transferred *solely* through this proven methodology of instruction. It is primarily achievable, however, because the instrument is *external* to the player, which is of critical importance.

The operatic instrument, by greatest contrast, is part of the little understood human body not, as yet, created by man. The workings of the fragile and inscrutable vocal cords have always remained elusive. For these reasons, very few sons and daughters of opera singers follow in their parent's shadows as little is transferable through nature or nurture. *Opera* is music's *great equalizer* where no direct line is generally traceable and where one finds no vocal equivalent of a Dorothy DeLay**. To further confuse and complicate matters, what may work well for one singer can be downright disastrous for another; one artist's vocal *teacher* is another's voice *terminator.*

*LATIN "without which, nothing!"
**Famous Juilliard violin teacher whose pupils include Perlman, Sonnenberg-Salerno among many other world-class violinists.

Many legendary singers (Caruso, Olivero, et al) were once told to get *real jobs*. Others (Corelli, Del Monaco, et al), recognizing early on that their *prestigious* teachers were literally *ruining* their voices, listened to their own bodies and went their own way with uniquely glorious results. More than a few major singers (Pinza, et al) did not read a solitary note of music. These situations are neither relevant nor possible when the instruments are external to the body.

We can now perhaps begin to understand why some will say that they like classical music **excepting** *opera*. Two types of voices are particularly unwelcome to vulnerably innocent ears: the large sound produced via *forcing* and the light voiced *girlish warbler* so inaccurately termed a *coloratura soprano* (see Glossary). There is much less variation in the techniques, tones and overall sound of pianists and violinists than is the case with opera singers where the differences can be downright startling. It is of vital importance, therefore, that a first experience be at least minimally pleasing to the ear if not the eye since, as with other initial ventures, one desires repetition if pleasurable and, conversely, recoils if painful. Nowhere is this basic psychological analogy more apt than with respect to the art and science– or dramatic lack thereof– of opera singing.

As a former *pop-culture* example, an easily produced voice which uniquely embraces the auditory sense is that belonging to Frank Sinatra in his early prime. Though not openly announced, more than a few opera singers have *privately studied** the incomparable phrasing and the *ebb and flow* of Ol' Blue Eyes sound. Vocal teachers have scholarly words for these– *legato* (a tying together), *portamento* (a gliding), and *rubato* (literally to *rob* rhythmically). I would be surprised, however, if the young Sinatra really knew– or much cared– what these terms meant as I suspect that his technique was essentially intuitive, based on his *feel* of the music which was instantly and deeply transferred to the emotional receptors of his listeners.

*This is also true of classical trumpeters who *observed* Louis Armstrong.

It is no coincidence, consequently, that most of Sinatra's rivals of the 1940's and 50's, many with wider ranges and stronger voices, have receded to obscurity while he has achieved rare vocal immortality.

So, just how does one build a bridge from the sound of Sinatra to the operatic *bellowing bull* or *fluttering finch*? The answer, emphatically, is that one does not and should not. The solution is to proceed, in stages, from a Francis Albert to a semi-operatic voice – heard in productions such as *Phantom...*, *Les Miserables*, or the recent and plentiful neo-nostalgic revivals of *Show Boat*, *South Pacific*, *Brigadoon*, et al – to the beautifully produced opera voice such as Björling's or Tebaldi's. This *stepping-stone* approach also *conditions* to further interest without any underlying sense of cringing fear. And, so importantly, the trip should never be taken from a *puddle* to an *ocean*, as a *lake* will do just fine (specific recommendations for particularly idyllic lakes are given in Chapter 16). *Opera*, that unique comprehensive vocal art form, imposes an auditory and a visual experience where, if there is no *listen*, there will certainly also be no *look* on the living stage.

As dramatically delineated at the beginning of this chapter, damage can be done rapidly and permanently. Fortunately, *opera aversion* is a preventable childhood disease if parents are aware of the recommended immunization. Vaccinations are widely available.

7 - "Sorry, No Comprendo"

The preceding chapters dealt with the two major barriers to a deeper appreciation of the form known as *opera* and, though single entities, they tend to closely align with particularly aversive effect.

This brief chapter seeks to completely dispel an entirely illusory hurdle, that being non-fluent in the language of the work's *libretto* precludes any hope of enjoying the wonderful vocal art. The vast bulk of standard repertory operas are in Italian, French, German or Russian. With great regularity, I have been told that not knowing the language has always been a repelling force and my response has always been that no such requirement exists. Allow me to offer potent historical evidence in this regard.

In the 1950's and early 60's, Rudolph Bing*, with some reluctance, produced some of the more popular operas (*La Bohème*, *Carmen*, *Così Fan Tutte*, et al) in English. There was never a better time to so experiment as Bing had, at his disposal, the greatest array of native born talent since the opera house opened some 75 years before**. The parents of these first generation American artists came from Europe, Russia– the usual places– around the turn of the 20th century, mainly during its first decade. The bulk of the *home grown glories*, in all categories, came of vocal age in mid-century, following a legendary few such as Rosa Ponselle and Lawrence Tibbett who had permanently paved this road a generation before.

What occurred, however, was that the audiences and broadcast listeners– many of whom had jumped on the *opera in English* bandwagon– didn't like the result. First, it was difficult to understand the *English* words due to the nature of the production of many operatic voices.

---

*Bing was General Manager of New York City's Metropolitan Opera from 1950-72. This tenure was the second longest, exceeded only by Giulio Gatti-Casazza who presided there from 1908-35.
**See Ch. 15 for a more detailed discussion of this area.

Additionally, many felt that the *flow of the line* was disrupted in these translations. If one, then, cannot readily comprehend the words in native English, why not just continue to produce the work in the language in which it was written? Why not, indeed!

If even a rudimentary understanding of a foreign language is not necessary, just what is required for a basic appreciation of this vocal art form? An open mind, and ear, and the following of a basic sequence of steps (Chapter 16). As this book is intended as a preparatory primer for those who do not *yet* know that they will come to love *opera*, the simple sequence is important and is now previewed:

> ♪ Read the stories *first* (they can equally appeal to young people). In fact, a well written and illustrated child's book is suitable for all age groups* as these tales cover the gamut of human emotion. Many read as do Biblical stories and some are just that (i.e. *Samson and Delilah*, *Salome*, et al). I recommend that no music be listened to at this point. Years ago, I suggested a review of the *libretto* at this point so the novice could closely follow the action at various stages in the work. This, however, has been rendered less necessary by the modern opera video on VHS or DVD. (A specific recommended order is offered in Chapter 16). The best of these are ideal in terms of acting as well as singing, the lavish backgrounds enhancing the overall experience and, most fortunately, subtitles are concise, well timed and unobtrusive.

In summary, this *obstacle* is not only transparent but non-existent, the operatic *wizard behind the curtain*. Though surely desirable for an in-depth study of the great vocal art form, not one word of any foreign language is necessary for our current purposes. Familiarity with the story and the attendant stage action is all that you need– the composer and the singers will take it from there.

> ### "No Comprendo" is "No Problema"!

*My personal preference is Stories of the World's Great Operas by Thomas Matthews (illus. by Robert Shore), Golden Press, New York, 1968. Used book stores are excellent sources for this work and opera books in general.

Part III

"The Wonderful Domino Effect"

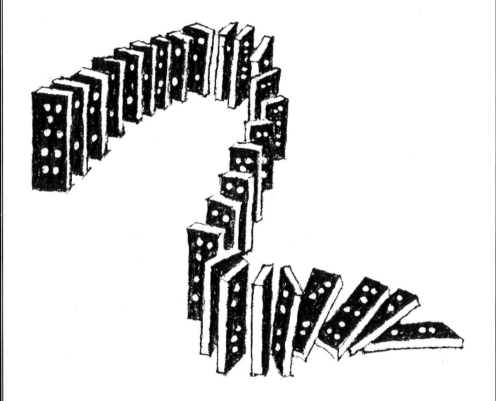

8 - The Offer I Couldn't Refuse

As Chapter 4 probably receded from consciousness by now, what with such unwelcome interferences by *arrogant opera goers* and *aural child abusers*, a quick memory jog seems in order. While life went on in the *Nation's Oldest City*, I continued to be plagued by *Gorin-guilt*.

We made some wonderful later in life friends here, the kind who, like us, chose to simplify, to reorder priorities, and to touch some lives in the few years remaining to us this time around. At *exactly* the time that I offered my *child* up to that Jacksonville studio altar, a musically eclectic local college radio station commenced broadcasting here. Initially manned only by students, it became immediately apparent that "Batch" and "Choppin" would not pass muster in the classical format. One or two more mature community volunteers soon appeared who could, at the very least, approximate proper pronunciation. One of our new friends, a professor at the college, hosted a weekly program in which she had local guests discuss the varied arts and cultural events. Fascinated by my record collection, knowledge, and passion for *opera*, she asked that I be her guest, bring a few of my *kids* in and brag. What proud *parent* could refuse? Gathering up a few Caruso classics, into the studio I marched, put on a large pair of earphones, and felt as surprisingly comfortable behind that microphone as I always have discussing *opera* with so many for so long. I was at such ease because I was firmly ensconced in my one *cloud nine zone–* OPERA. I would discuss areas such as early acoustic recording, how *modern* Caruso's voice sounded while most of his colleagues seemed archaic and, generally, anything that struck my fancy at the time. It must have gone over well as I kept being invited back rather regularly for sequels.

After the fifth such appearance, the station manager called me in and proposed that I consider my own three hour weekly program. My immediate declination was explained in terms of there being no audience for *opera* in this community. "You're wrong!" was his less than subtle reply as he flatly explained to me that what occurred following my guest appearances were rarely encountered in his broadcasting career: he received consistent telephone calls and mail encouraging him to include me in the stations format. He asked only that I give it *a bit more thought.*

Truth be told, I thought of nothing else. My *own* opera radio program! Almost immediately, it dawned on me with the sound of a hammer on an anvil that I could now have the elusive answers to the riddles: I felt like a reincarnated "Calaf" in *Turandot.* "When was the last time you played that record?" NOW! "What are you going to do with all those records?" SHARE THEM WITH MY LISTENERS! *My listeners.* What a ring to it. A new meaning for *squillo**. Those answers, which have evaded so many passionate record collectors since Edison's *cylinder reproducing machine* of 1877, could be mine in this moment, in this place and time.

I didn't have to *think about it* very long. A very comforting statement by the station manager was that the imposing looking console at the little studio was "...nothing more than a big stereo system"; he must have noticed in my demeanor that I seemed awed by the equipment. Was he right! I did the necessary technical training and I was ready to go next Monday. Last minute jitters hit me and I scheduled a final run through on Thursday. As requested, I brought the actual LP's that I would play on the very first *The Joy of Opera* in just four days.

THURSDAY: 11:40 a.m.– "Are you ready?" asked the station manager as he informed me that I'm on in 20 minutes. He's got it terribly wrong: it's 96 *hours* not 20 *minutes*. He went on to explain to me that the student host called in sick and I was the only broadcaster here...*Broadcaster?* *Me?* The *only* one here? *20 minutes*?! It all converged on me now, the entire surrealistic unraveling of order when I most needed it- the opera addiction, the passion, the *coincidences*, and now that terribly premature MOMENT where one steps up to that plate and swings, where one makes great love or doesn't, where one *better* know what one is talking about, what one *is* about, what one IS!

---

*Squillo literally relates to the resonant striking of a bell. In opera parlance, it is the *thrill* one gets listening to certain voices with *metal* which produce *ring, ping* or *goosebumps.*

"The Brilliant Shooting Stars" I was going to call it 96 hours hence, but now it was down to 15 minutes and depleting. Anita Cerquetti, Flaviano Labò, Ettore Bastianini, and three tenors who never celebrated their 40th birthdays– Josef Schmidt, Fritz Wunderlich, and Mario Lanza. (Yes indeed, the very same Lanza who was part of the Brody/Fontana duels of four decades earlier before that *Swedish guy Björling* changed everything.) Other than the Hollywood idol of the 1950's, who were these names I was featuring on my inaugural radio program?

They were, so luminescently, those *instant flashes* we were allowed to cherish for that "...one brief, shining moment." The tenor Labò had a reasonably long operatic career on the stage, but I included him because he, so strangely, made a miniscule handful of recordings in the studio. The one I featured– recorded in 1957– is highly prized and, to my knowledge, has not been transferred to the CD format. A statement that would soon go over the air was "you may not know the name, but you'll never forget the voice." But something happened first, immediately after I pushed a half-inch switch forward– the "On Air" switch– as time ran out on me.
"GOOD AFTERNOON, WFCF OPERA LOVERS, CURRENT AND FUTURE."

No great catastrophe followed though I caught myself "*ah-ah'ing*" a good few times, but that was about the worst of it. My training on the two top-line turntables paid off, where a half turn backwards allowed a *dragless* start of the music a clean one second after I stopped talking. One by one, I showcased these great voices with relevant bio information: Cerquetti (career only a scant 10 years), Labò (studio recordings rarer than snow in Florida), Bastianini (died of throat cancer in his prime), Schmidt (barely five feet in height and who died at 38 in an internment camp during WWII), Wunderlich (died at 35 just before heralded Met debut in a household accident), and Lanza (died in Rome in 1959 at 38 under circumstances of continuing mystery).

The phone rang and a woman thanked me for the new program and asked how come she had never heard of these thrilling singers before (for a moment I almost felt *personally* responsible).

She added that she got *the chills* from Cerquetti's great voice (she felt the *cutting edge* on an elemental level). A few minutes later, another call as a man thanked me for a novel *approach* adding that the obscure Labò had one of the greatest voices that he had ever heard. Just what *approach* did he refer to? I would think of this much later on. At least five calls were received during this initial *The Joy of Opera* and not one requested that this guy with the Brooklyn accent be taken off the air. A gentleman was deeply moved by the tragic saga of the tiny tenor Schmidt, and noted an inherent sadness in the voice itself: I almost jumped for joy when he said that as I felt the exact same thing since I first heard that sound four decades before. This man, however, had never heard of Josef Schmidt until a few *minutes* ago. So it was indeed true: he didn't know the *name* but he'll never forget the *voice*. As the program approached its conclusion, I truly experienced *joy* in sharing the first *The Joy of Opera* with listeners to whom I already felt a bond. The *baptism by fire* was over and I was home free in one piece. The station manager was smiling, shook my hand and told me that he received a call from a listener who found the new opera program *different*: I guess he, too, referred to my *approach*, whatever that was. I told him of the calls I received during the program. "Was I right?" "Yes, indeed!"

Several cards and letters awaited me when I arrived the following week, most of them specifically mentioning my fresh *approach*. I was benignly confused in the nicest possible way, but confused nonetheless. Just what *was* this *approach* so regularly perceived by MY LISTENERS?

The themes of the early *The Joy of Opera* programs included a format I originally called "The Great Unknowns" – later changed to "Rescues from the Dustbin,"* keeping great voices alive as long as possible. This group included a young Hungarian tenor Miklos Gafni who made one 10-inch LP around 1950. I always prized this disc, probably for the memory of my mother bringing it home after Mr. Seidman (the local record maven on Bay Parkway) told her

---

*Refers to the proverbial *dustbin of history*.

that he is the next *couldn't miss* tenor star. Gafni *missed* and missed badly though I never knew why until I received a call from a man who was the tenor's agent at the time (do you believe this one?) and he told me that Gafni was extremely difficult to deal with, a *primo uomo* in the most negative sense of the word.* I have continued this *rescue* theme to this day.

"Opera Rarities and Oddities" was particularly well received. Among the *oddest* was a 1908 Victor recording in which Geraldine Farrar jibes the great Caruso singing "he's had a highball" in clear English instead of the intended line "Si, per la vita" (yes, for life) from Puccini's *Madama Butterfly*.

Speaking of Caruso, I played a recording from his first session (1902) in which he comes in much too early and audibly exclaims "uh, uh" when he realized he was *dead* in the musical waters. From a movie soundtrack, I shared a very cautious Frank Sinatra in a duet with Kathryn Grayson from Mozart's *Don Giovanni*. And, rather unpleasant to the ears, Enrico Caruso Jr. gave us "Che Gelida Manina" from Puccini's *La Bohème*, in no way challenging his legendary father, let alone the magical Björling recording that began this whole adventure. I ended the program with a 1920 recording of the nine year old Jussi, a rarity only recently discovered. Also included was a 1904 recording of Moreschi, the last of the *castrati*, who was a member of the Sistine Chapel Choir.

At least once a month, I built into the program an in-depth analysis of complete operas, employing relevant recorded examples. And, since 1995, the last program of each month is devoted to listener requests.

Also in 1995, during one of my *rescue* formats, I showcased Igor Gorin– unfortunately via cassette– and recounted the sad saga of that lamented 12-inch Urania LP which I donated in response to the request of the lady from Palm Coast. A few minutes later the phone rang and a woman told me how much she was enjoying this program and added that *she* was that caller several years earlier. Wow!

---

*Italian. *first man*, the male counterpart to *prima donna* (first lady)

The *volcano* of listener response was a program I called "The *Four* Tenors: The Titans of Tenors." It was not possible a dozen or so years ago to turn on a public TV station and not hear the so-called *Three Tenors* (Luciano Pavarotti, Placido Domingo and Jose Carreras). Soon to follow this marketing bonanza was *Three Tenors II, III*, etc. Not yet out of steam, there was still room for the *Three Irish Tenors*, *Three Mo' Tenors* and *Three Cantors*. As the format was further squeezed, pushed, pulled, and twisted for any remaining commercially viable substance, the more it all distanced itself from music. I made it very clear during my program that the subtitle of this theme should be "one man's opinion." I then proceeded to offer my personal candidates for the title of *greatest tenor of the century*: Enrico Caruso (1873-1921), Lauritz Melchior (1890-1972), Jussi Björling (1911-1960) and Franco Corelli (1921-2003). I played some of their greatest recordings and gave my personal reasons for placing them on the *Mt. Rushmore of Opera*. No program elicited so many calls and mail, a few expressing *pique* as to how I could have left out Beniamino Gigli, Richard Tucker, Jan Peerce, et al, despite the fact that, during the program, I mentioned several times that my choices should in no way be equated with *brain surgery* or *rocket science*. Most disturbing to me, however, was the fact that there were actually a few out there who may have truly believed that *opera* did not exist before the advent of The Three Tenors.

I knew I received a lot of mail on a regular basis but I was floored when the station manager informed me that the response was greater than not only other classical broadcasters but jazz, rock, new age and alternative as well. Why was this? There was a general pattern to the cards and letters in which listeners thanked me for making it all so palatable, for explaining opera in particularly comprehensible terms. Several hinted that I was "turning them into opera lovers" and no comment would ever gratify me more. What I knew for sure was that it had to be more than a Brooklyn accent and the incorrect insertion of "r's" into words which didn't have them, and omitting them from those that did.

Any personal confusion that remained would soon dissipate when a listener– who surely didn't have to tell me who I wasn't– told me who I was with resounding simplicity. We are, however, one chapter premature.

9 - Opera's 'Regular Guy'

Over time, I had to reluctantly admit that I do possess some verbal attributes which are perceived by many ears as a *Brooklyn accent*. A few people thought they *nailed* me as a New Englander and tried to zero in on whether it was Connecticut, Massachusetts (usually Boston) or New Hampshire. I recall that three people asked what county in Ireland I called home and, one each, inquired about Italy or Greece. Susan always gets a hearty chuckle when these queries surface. In a sense, it kind of makes me feel rather *universal* which, come to think of it, is much the same with *opera*. What is absolutely clear, however, is that, for better or worse, my speaking voice is dramatically identifiable.

Consider the following as cases in point:

- ♪ Walking, and talking, with my wife, a jogger turns as she passes us and says "good show last week." She never broke stride.
- ♪ Leaving a physician's office, a lady in the adjoining waiting room states: "Mr. Brody, you don't know us but we know you well. Thank you for *The Joy of Opera* which brought back so many wonderful memories for my husband and me."
- ♪ In a local Radio Shack, I barely got out the words "I'm looking for some small speakers..." when the salesman extended his right hand, relating how happy he was to meet me personally, and added how much he has learned from my formats.

The essence of all this turned particularly fortuitous when, overhearing me conversing with an attendee at a local social event, a gentleman graciously interrupted and noted that my voice was *unmistakable*: within seconds, almost to the sound of *eureka*, he had me pegged, and thanked me for greatly deepening his appreciation of *opera* because I removed the *stuffiness* for him.

43

"And you know what?" he added, followed by a pointed pause, "you're a *regular guy*." A REGULAR GUY! There it was and it had the defining feel of a Wagnerian chord. "**Jumpin' Igarrophant!**" On the most basic level, that pause and statement drove home what I've always viscerally known: that, by long held general perception, one could not really be an *opera expert* AND a *regular guy*. You could be one OR the other, but not *both*. It was utterly eloquent in its simplicity. With that statement, I curiously felt as if he were a General pinning a medal of honor on my chest.

I usually react to things long after they occur, but not this time. Shaking his hand, I asked for, and gleefully received, his *permission* for the rights to that moniker *Opera's 'Regular Guy'*.

And that's the way it was, is and always will be as long as I feel **joy** in *The Joy of Opera*.

10 - The Spinoffs

In my own microcosmic fashion, I followed in the shadow of the growing list of trimorphs onto Spinoff Boulevard.

About three years into *The Joy of Opera*, I received a call from a woman who began by telling me that she recently heard my program, thought my *approach* "listener friendly," and asked if I would consider teaching for Elderhostel, of which she was the regional coordinator. Her tone, however, had a veiled impatience to it and, with an odd sense of vulnerability, I asked what *Elderhostel* was just a split second before yielding to a strong impulse to summarily decline. Her explanation was rapid and I only managed to pick up kernels of the operation, but two things she said struck me: that some instructors, possessing the very highest educational qualifications, have failed to resonate with the *hostelers* and that a *passionate familiarity* with one's subject area is paramount. It quickly dawned on me that the big difference here would be that these worldly people shall face me live, where I couldn't hide behind "Mikey" and, indeed, there is a wonderfully comforting sense of security in radio. True, I have performed before audiences since childhood, but this would be new; what convinced me to give it a try, though, was the policy of *dipping* a new instructor into *a survival training pool*, a one hour presentation rather than the full week format of one and one-half hours for five days where, as I would later witness, a good few credentialed scholars were totally devoured and not even a trace of their shattered egos was ever found again.

My subject, immediately chosen, would be *Caruso and the Gramophone* which clearly has remained the *softest* of my *security blankets*. In Brooklyn College, 40 years before, I used the same subject for my pedagogy speech although I did not *then* opt to teach. A vivid memory of that tense affair was when one of the five judging professors asked me "...just what does *ffrr* denote on the London LP label?" His disappointment was almost painfully palpable when I said "full frequency range recording" as, clearly, the anticipated response was to be "I don't know, Sir." Though it never mattered, I passed nonetheless.

Yes, *Caruso and the Gramophone* it would again be. No opera singer ever had more influence on an industry and a century: Enrico Caruso, born in the 19th, still *sells* in the 21st. More books and papers have been written of him than of any other singer in history. One of the more curious was authored by Dr. P. Mario Marafioti, the tenor's Otolaryngologist in New York.*

To fit into just one hour, I recorded– on audio cassette– a representative sample of the totally unique voice and how it changed so remarkably from 1902 through its last session in 1920. The selections simultaneously demonstrated the evolution of sound recording in the first two decades of the 20th century. In contrast to three years before, I was now downright eager to take this show *on the road*.

With 50 receptive seniors did I share my comfort zone and the hour was up in a flash. What received the most positive reaction was when I played one of the tenor's three recorded "Sextets" from *Lucia di Lammermoor,* before which I pointed out how *modern* Caruso's voice would sound while the other five would seem almost *prehistoric* in contrast. This sonic magic will probably never be adequately understood, yet it only partially explains why the name "Caruso" will stand out among all the other stentorian titans as long as opera singing is valued.

I knew I went over well from the outset and the *flocking* to me at the conclusion of the presentation confirmed it. Elderhostel students submit rating sheets with comments and, a few weeks later, I received the most gratifying score of 4.93 (5 is perfect) with truly heart warming accompanying sentiments. Goodness, all I did was share my passion, but I would soon learn that this is *the* vital ingredient, rendering all others, quite literally, academic.

Caruso's Method of Voice Production, Dover Publications, Inc., New York, 1949

I was immediately engaged for several standard courses and, about a year later, another university hired me for their Elderhostel program. This was becoming almost a full time position now but not, in any fashion, a *job*. I really was "turning people into opera lovers" because they told me so. Though not a formally religious person, I felt like a proselytizing musical minister zealously seeking conversions and I placed my piano *gigs* on the far back burner where they still remain.

My courses, with two exceptions, are operatic in focus. *The Highs and Lows of Opera: A Glass Shattering Experience* covers the categories and subcategories of voice– with spectacular recorded examples– from the highest *soprano* to the lowest *basso*. *Carmen and the Italian Verismo* traces the great influence of Bizet's masterpiece on the Italian *realism* operas which would follow 15 years later. Others included *Verdi and Wagner* and *The Bel Canto Period of Italian Opera*.

An illuminating question asked during one of these courses concerned my opinion of "...the art of Elvis Presley." Without thought or delay, I responded that "I missed him" (as in "...two ships passing in the night"). The ascent of *The King*– but not my sovereign– coincided exactly with that *Swedish Guy* inflaming my auditory senses and thirst for vast knowledge operatic. Accordingly, despite my otherwise fitting age group, Elvis had no relevance to me: thus my answer– to quote a truly immortal hero, the affable Sergeant Hans Schultz– was, and could only be, "I know nothing"!

Perhaps my most important effort in this context is the non-operatic *Beethoven: The Tormented Titan of Music*. My premise in this course is that Beethoven is the single most *influential* composer in the history of music, due primarily to his agonizing hearing loss. I make my case by an in-depth analysis of his changing music from around 1800 (when the problem was first noted) through 1808 when the composer had already shattered most of the musical boundaries that existed before he came of age. Though only 38 then, Beethoven had already thoroughly revolutionized instrumental music. The only other non-vocal course is *Historical Harmonies: Music of the First Coast* which traces the varied St. Augustine history strictly through its music.

As with *The Joy of Opera*, I began to receive mail at home via correspondence forwarded to me from both colleges, two comments of which stand out: "Where were you 50 years ago when I 'closed the door' on *opera*": and, from a man who signed up for the Elderhostel program *despite* the listed *opera* course, came "Dear Sir, now you have gone and done it." He went on to explain how deeply the course affected him and asked my assistance, which was lovingly offered, in making up for lost time and placing his operatic education on *fast-forward*. "Your enthusiasm is contagious," in those same four words, was written by several *hostelers*.

Now the *spinoffs* of the *spinoff* began. Would I do private opera seminars? *Yes, indeed!* For the St. Augustine Film Society, I pulled a *Leonard Bernstein* and previewed opera videos with my piano demonstrations of relevant themes, most recently for a superbly beautiful 1995 film of *Madama Butterfly,* presented in the United States by Martin Scorsese (Chapter 16).

One *spinner* even fulfilled a long dormant childhood fantasy of my being a pianist for silent movies. The Film Society began such a venture with an extravaganza of early 20th century St. Augustine, complete with period dress and antique cars. There they all were: Rudolph Valentino, Theda Bara (portrayed by Susan), Pearl White (Pauline, as in "perils of"), et al. The featured film, shot here in 1914, was a controversial *bombshell* called *A Florida Enchantment* which dealt with such subjects as *cross dressing* and *sex change* (yes, 1914). With minimal light, I improvised the score around an inane theme I believe I originally heard on the live *Soupy Sales Show* on very early TV.* At the extremely successful conclusion, many were shocked when I stood and they began to realize that I was *alive*.

Life was not boring in the historic old town as these functions joined *The Joy of Opera* as melodically meaningful usurpers of my time. In answer to Gershwin's musical question "who could ask for anything more?" – "Certainly not I!"

*The program must have been localized to the Northeast U. S. and, apparently, never made it westward to Oklahoma as Susan had absolutely no recollection of it.

11 - "The Lighting Director's Son"

As the second millennium Anno Domini took its final bow a few years ago, I thought it particularly appropriate to pay homage to its twentieth and last century, our first, and the glorious neo-nascent century of recording. To so honor, I devoted three consecutive radio programs, comprising seven and one-half hours, to that truly remarkable history of sound reproduction and its several leaps forward.

Although primitive foil and wax cylinders existed in the last decades of the nineteenth century, recording of *high brow* music began in earnest around 1900. Edison himself had doubted any lasting future for music on his 1877 *cylinder reproducing machine* which he called the *phonograph*. Slowly, but surely, did the *flat disc* (less cumbersome and much easier to reproduce) become standard. Designed to be played on a *gramophone*, these 78 RPM* rubber, metal but mostly shellac platters proliferated. From the outset, it was the operatic voice that held center stage, first with piano accompaniment and, after 1905, an *orchestra* comprised of a handful of musicians was added. There was no certainty then that this fledgling industry would survive. In Europe, the Gramophone and Typewriter Company (G&T), sounding like it was hedging its bets on the technological future, would soon affiliate with The Victor Talking Machine Company here. In 1902, the G&T front office forbade Fred Gaisberg, its European executive, to record a young Italian tenor who requested too high a fee. Gaisberg, the vocal visionary, ignored the edict and the voice of the 29-year-old Enrico Caruso was emblazoned on wax and shellac for the first time, simultaneously launching the unique recording revolution.

*78 RPM was a compromised standard measure of recording speed. Of the 229 Caruso recordings for Victor between 1904 and 1920, speeds ranged from 74.23 to 81.82 RPM with the vast majority recorded around 76RPM.

My three programs illustrated the significant mileposts with riveting recorded examples from the earliest attempts, the electrical age circa 1925, the sublime convenience of the microgroove 33⅓ long playing record of 1948*, the stereophonic age around 1956, and the digital CD some 25 years later.

A few weeks after these programs aired, a detailed letter arrived at my home. The writer, a sound engineer by training, began by telling me how meaningful my programs had been to him, especially the last three. He mentioned that "...perhaps..." his family's history may be of interest. In this understatement, he went on to relate that his mother was a member of the Metropolitan Opera's *Corps de Ballet* in the second decade of the last century, where she met his father who came there as an 18-year-old apprentice in 1908 and retired from that venerable shrine as the Chief Lighting Director in 1954. He went on to describe the numerous gifts given to his parents: cuff links from Beniamino Gigli, a mechanical cigarette box from Maria Jeritza, stemware from Lily Pons, letters from the Melchiors, et al. Also, and not generally known, Caruso was widely praised as a caricaturist who nervously sketched the ballerinas before a performance and gave the finished product to them as a gift. The writer's mother, regarding these as worthless *doodles*, disposed of them. Needless to say, the art work of the great tenor is rare and coveted. The letter was signed "...your devoted listener, Ted Buchter."

Strangely, the name Buchter rang a distant bell and it didn't take too long to find the reference in one of my favorite books *Requiem for a Yellow Brick Brewery*** (a derisive name given to the then new Met in 1883 by the flamboyant impresario COL. James Henry Mapleson).

*THANK YOU COLUMBIA for allowing us to relax for twenty-three minutes instead of four and one-half. Actually, RCA Victor introduced a wide groove long playing record in the early 1930s which did not succeed.
**John Briggs, Little, Brown & Company, 1969, Boston and Toronto.

What I could not get out of my consciousness were the dates of the Lighting Director's tenure: Jacob Buchter was hired in 1908 (the first year of the regime of Giulio Gatti-Casazza) and retired five years into the Rudolph Bing era almost five decades later. My goodness, almost 50 years in that hallowed house in which he witnessed the two most glittering golden ages of any opera house in the 20th century.

A few weeks later, simply unable to get the unlikely script of the Buchters' out of my mind, I called Ted and invited him to be a guest on *The Joy of Opera*, unusual as these weekly programs are essentially spontaneous. His response was that he did not wish to impede the flow of my program and asked, in the most sincere tone, whether I really thought he had "…anything to contribute?" Sensing that he felt successful in squirming off that *hook*, I only asked that he give it a bit more thought as I, totally out of character, resorted to that insidious technique known as the *guilt trip* and, as is usual, it worked like that proverbial *charm*. Ted Buchter's appearances have received as much positive listener feedback as any of my programs since the inaugural in 1993.

Ted still speaks of my radio efforts rekindling precious memories and how privileged he feels. I still speak of the wonder of that *coincidence of convergence* and my privilege in linking with The Lighting Director's Son in this place and time. In the end, I guess we are indeed two particularly privileged *regular guys* who, like everyone else, aren't getting any younger! When so magic a moment came our way, in so insecure an age, we grabbed it and we cherished it.

Part IV

"... current and future"

12 - Sanitized Opera in the Digital Age

> *"The thrill is gone–*
> *The thrill is gone away."*
> *–BB King*

<u>July, 1993: Long Branch, NJ</u>

"What errors do you want obliterated"? asked the sound engineer after I completed, in one continuous take as hoped, the first of my piano recordings. Though 57 at the time, and surely should have known by then, I wondered just how this *obliteration* process would be accomplished since, being a remnant of what truly felt like an earlier *aeon*, I still believed that *what's done is done*. Clearly confused by my confusion, the technician demonstrated how the computer's *cursor* simply eliminates any *offending* note and replaces it with a single corrected *plinked* strike. Stating that I could live comfortably with my unique imperfections, I declined the offer of alteration yet a riveting thought persisted– are errors *out* these days? Please consider three more related personal experiences:

♪ The next hint of my unreadiness for the beckoning brave new high-tech 21st century came when the unthinkable was confirmed, that a *computer* was the *soul-less* soloist in a mechanically perfect performance of Beethoven's *"Pathetique" Piano Sonata* which I heard in one of those upscale stores in San Francisco.

♪ Similarly, I heard a most *proficient* electronic keyboardist, the hotel entertainer for the evening. In this same time frame, I was refusing offers– and losing income– if a *real* piano was unavailable for weddings, private parties, and other events. When he took a break, I complimented him on his skill, told him who I was and asked his advice on *non-acoustic* instruments (meaning that there better be an electric outlet around). Almost *proudly*, he told me that he was a *finger syncher* and that he "...couldn't play six chords..." and graciously demonstrated how the *computer* performed in an endless array of tones and rhythms.

♪ And, finally, in an interesting group conversation along these lines, a gentleman asked, with sincerity, if talent was *obsolete*?

What, you may be thinking, has any of this to do with *opera*? I beg your indulgence for the remaining pages of this chapter.

Most of my readers of Medicare eligibility age who lived in New York City in the 1950's should fondly remember WEVD, that unique multi-language radio station. One of their programs, and my favorite, was an Italian Opera show called *L'Ugola D'Oro* (The Golden Throat) which showcased a different singer each day; I can still so vividly recall the Act One prelude to *La Traviata* as the opening and closing theme. One afternoon, listening with half an ear, the host announced "...il tenore Franco Corelli," a name not known to me. As I gradually focused onto the unusually vibrant voice, shrouded in poor sound quality, my mind conjured up another WW II vintage Italian tenor who, for reasons unknown, somehow didn't make much of an international *splash*. By the end of the segment, now in rapt attention, I just couldn't understand how this one *missed* with such a pensively sensual flowing sound which was solidly baritonal in the lower register, yet thrillingly brilliant in the upper which included C's and C#'s. In short, this truly astonishing voice was something very rare; indeed, it recalled a bygone era of vocal style.

Without delay, I went to Forzano & Fleri, my special record store on Mulberry Street in New York City's *Little Italy* and asked my maven about the *old tenor* Corelli. "Non vecchio, e giovane" (He's young, not old) was simultaneously accompanied by the excited pulling of a few 78s (no, they did *not* go gently into that *good night*) along with some 10 and 12-inch LPs, all on the Italian

Cetra label. I couldn't wait to get 'em on the turntable. I also felt somewhat vindicated because Cetra's sound in the mid 1950's was about a decade behind its London and Angel counterparts in Europe, not to speak of our domestic RCA Victor and Columbia. So, here we were in 1956 or '57, in a moment of unique convergence, when the half century old 78 and the pre-teen 45 (on the way out in classical) finally ceded the stage to the *new king*, the monaural 33⅓ microgroove long-playing record now joined by its new born stereophonic sibling.

At home now, the voice of the *giovane* was ready for my full attention. The room was immediately filled with a vibrant resonance that was uniquely special. I felt that I had struck *gold* and I wanted not only to stake my claim but also to share the wealth. but I waited awhile. But how would this sound translate in the Met? The *Met*? Corelli wasn't even on their roster. Since the advent of electrical recording (circa 1925), opera fans have often been very disappointed with *gramo-genic** voices which somehow didn't *cut it* in their cherished theaters. Every new *phenom* immediately went through the grapevine of the *cognoscenti* (the knowers) to determine how he or she sounds *in the house*.

I waited, but there were only occasional mentions of Corelli's name, even though he was *the* rising star in La Scala and other major European houses. I then took preemptive action and, sometime in 1958, I wrote letters to the Metropolitan Opera Association and Capitol Records informing them of my *strike*. I chose Capitol (EMI) for a specific reason: London had del Monaco and several younger contemporaries, Angel had di Stefano, RCA had Björling, and Columbia had Tucker. In addition, Capitol was beginning to record complete operas but, as it would turn out, not for very long.

The responses to my letters were dramatically different in tone (Appendices B & C). The detachment of the Met's *Opera News* editor stood in stark contrast to the excited familiarity of the Capitol executive who assured me that Corelli was being closely scrutinized.

*Reminder- Phono-Genic (from *phonograph*) technically refers to the *cylinder.* the name *"phonograph"* was applied in 1877 by Thomas A. Edison himself.

Indeed he must have been since he was simultaneously signed by EMI (but on their Angel label where Corelli, in effect, totally replaced the rapidly vocally declining Giuseppe di Stefano) and engaged by the Metropolitan Opera. The framed responses hang, side-by-side, on the wall in my music room.

Franco Corelli made his debut on January 27, 1961 in Verdi's *Il Trovatore*, the occasion also marking the 60th anniversary of the composer's death. In a once in a lifetime dose of good fortune, it also marked the debut of Leontyne Price. Also in the cast were Robert Merrill and the mezzo-soprano Irene Dalis.*

Sitting in the furthest most reaches of the Met's *Family Circle*– as far back as one can get while still within the confines of the building– was your author. The performance still lingers in the memory and Corelli's voice even surpassed the recordings. Yet, things would become *indelible* a month later when, after a 35 year absence, Bing restaged Puccini's *Turandot*. The work, despite a strong cast, did not ignite in 1926 but Bing, against advice, *knew* that he had, in Corelli and Birgit Nilsson, the ideal protagonists for the two heroic major roles, and he was not going to allow this *once in a century* opportunity to pass him by. Nobody attending that now legendary performance will ever forget it. Over a full orchestra, the sound of that *tenor* and *soprano* vying for vocal supremacy was indescribable and I have not since heard such tones emanate from human throats. An astounding thing occurred during this performance; I experienced a *sympathetic resonance* of Corelli's voice to some of the steel beams in the wall to my right. After the performance I mentioned this to *the old timer*– every major opera house has one– who heartily agreed, adding that "Melchior did it too." There is a word to describe this effect – THRILL!

---

*In a 1999 Elderhostel, two of my senior students wondered if the name Irene Dalis– their family friend– meant anything to me. "Yes, indeed it did!" After a search, I sent them a copy of the review of the 1961 performance and a cassette of one of my favorite radio programs suggesting that they share it with Ms. Dalis. A few weeks later, a rich-voiced caller identified herself as the mezzo telling me that her first thought was "no way in heck" was she going to listen to yet another opera broadcaster. She did it anyway and found my approach different and exciting. I love when this kind of thing happens.

Yes, THRILL! It appears most unlikely, my dear younger readers, that you will ever experience that elemental chill to the spine that I have just described and, for this loss, I feel for you. What is so different now? Have things changed that much from the immediate post WW II years, from the 1950's and early 60's?

Ooooh, Yeah! Perhaps the earliest sign of it was a barely perceptible shift of emphasis from vocals to visuals. Remember the shaky, shabby sets where doors didn't open, where only the handle of the sword emerged from the sheath, and the myriad other less than perfect such moments? If not, it will remain only in our collective memory as it almost never occurs these days. How did this happen? Did someone recently receive *divine* instruction in stagecraft? No, a decision was made, in this most expensive of all the arts, to transfer the *big budget bucks* to the areas of the visual and special effects. Hollywood already paved the road with Todd-A-O, Cinemascope, Cinerama and PanaVision; *opera* was over a decade behind and it didn't want to lose any more ground as the public's eyes, quite literally, were opened.

For most of the last full century, a flimsily built junk door that didn't properly open, may have elicited a few chuckles which quickly faded when the great voices began to swell. Now, however, that jammed door and swordless handle were deemed entirely unacceptable, indeed, *verboten.*

As with that hapless frog who immediately jumped out of a pot of warm water, only to silently allow himself to be boiled alive with an incremental increase of temperature from a cold water start, the shift from ear to eye was gradual but inexorable. Only a scant few noticed but I was one of them, and by the early 1970's, I felt that something was changing but I couldn't then *nail* it. I also felt something else– isolation– but not, mercifully, for too long.

The first sign of a change came in the Met broadcasts. Becoming aware that I was no longer devoting my 100% rapt attention to the performances, I gave 110% in trying to figure it out. Slowly, a picture began to develop.

There was a vague *cautiousness* to the singing, most evident in the more taxing major roles. But there was more: the new singers, making broadcast debuts, had a curious *sameness of sound* over and above the caution, the blander voices no longer immediately identifiable. The *voiceprints* were disappearing. My goodness, yet again: it happened in Hollywood and it spread to the opera house.

Finally, by the mid to late 1970's, I began to have supportive company and what company! That ageless operatic visionary Kitty Carlisle Hart wondered where, or *if*, the great voices of the future were being nurtured. She summarily refuted the *au currant* premise that the huge old houses, such as La Scala and the Met, were *passé* and unnatural for the human voice, noting the so many glorious *humans* who had little trouble filling those cavernous arenas for so long.

In 1977, Lou Cevetillo, music writer for the *Westchester-Rockland Newspapers*, zeroed in on whether too much money was being funneled to sets and costumes and not enough on encouraging and nourishing fine nascent voices. Quoting Corelli no less, Mr. Cevetillo noted it is far more important to "...hear a great voice than to see a realistic snowstorm."

At the same time, in an article entitled "The Met: Ghosts of Christmas Past," Manuela Hoelterhoff of the *Wall Street Journal* openly discussed the eroding vocal standards in stark juxtaposition to the *glitter* of the new visual opulence. She also resented the then current comfortable *chutzpah* of "...passing off second-stringers as major artists." Hoelterhoff concluded by nostalgically recalling the many singers who, when they "...stepped onto Bing's stage, stepped into history as well."

And, a little later, in two wonderfully detailed articles, Peter G. Davis of the *New York Times* delved into the waters of the now far more obvious shift. In "Where Are the Great Opera Singers of Tomorrow" (April 20, 1980), Davis focuses on the alarming lack of back-up to the shrinking star-level pool (the aging Sutherland, Caballé, Milnes, Pavarotti, and Domingo) and noted that even James Levine could not ignore the increasing scarcity of the *large-voiced* dramatic singer and found that standards like *Aida* and

Trovatore "...cannot be cast from strength." And, in "Twilight of the Opera Superstar" (March 15, 1981), Davis bluntly announces that "...we are likely witnessing a last gasp from the past, a veritable twilight of the gods." The *gods* referred to are the dwindling possessors of the great big voices with the *ring* and *ping* which gave so many of us those thrills, chills, and goosebumps for so long– i.e. the *squillo* effect.

In a most recent revelation of current reality, the Met almost admitted the shift by creating *repertory adjustments*. Melvyn Krauss, senior fellow at the Hoover Institution, Stanford University, hit the bullseye dead center. In his *Wall Street Journal* article of December 18, 2003 called "Opera Is Suffering From A Supply Side Crisis," Mr. Krauss was referring not to the economy, but to the lack of the supply of great voices, especially in the standard Italian repertory:

> "The recent passing of the great Italian tenor of the '50's and '60's, Franco Corelli, reminds us that not only are the glorious and glamorous voices like Mr. Corelli's absent from today's opera scene, but so, for want of suitable casting, are many of the operas in which Mr. Corelli and his contemporaries made their reputations."

WOW! He's talking about *La Forza del Destino, La Gioconda, Andrea Chenier*, and even reduced performances of *Aida*: shades of Maestro Levine a dozen years earlier. Krauss was by no means finished as he introduced an absolutely intriguing concept known as "cast proof productions." In an exceedingly expensive attempt at *sleight-of-sense*, the aim here is to stage performances that are visually "...so spectacular..." that "...the inferior singing is overlooked...". CAST PROOF PRODUCTIONS*? Yes, indeed– like a game of *Three-Card-Monte*, the quick maneuver from *ear* to *eye* was accomplished and most of us lost. When this *cat* was out of that *bag*, I felt the gloat of "I told you so" but said nothing for two reasons– nobody asked me, and I wasn't *then* writing this book.

---

*So expensive, however, are these productions that repertory adjustment has become the general solution to this reality.

Let me share one final graphic example. About five years ago, I did two consecutive programs to a theme I called "The Great American Baritone Relay Race" in which I discussed, with recorded examples, the unique uninterrupted passing of the baton from Richard Bonelli to Lawrence Tibbett to John Charles Thomas to Robert Weede to Leonard Warren to Robert Merrill to Cornell MacNeil to Sherrill Milnes. The reason for the length of this sentence is that it describes eight baritones spanning the vast bulk of the 20th century. They were distinctively diverse in their vocal timbre but all were assuredly *Verdi baritones**. Finally, in the 1980's, the stick was dropped and it was neither coincidental nor accidental, for the times, as we have just reviewed, were indeed *a' changin'.*

The most recent, and potentially most devastating component (hey there, was that another frog that just jumped into the pot of cold water) to the vanishing THRILL of the live experience concerns an ever shrinking piece of audio equipment possessing an increasingly sensitive membrane which is still called the *microphone.* Many of you probably recall a suspended *recording* mike which many opera companies used to capture their performances, some later authorized for release in conjunction with fund raisers, commemoratives, or other significant occasions. Some of these sanctioned live treasures have become legendary and the sound, for the most part, was– and still is– quite fine for the time since *mike* was optimally positioned for these specific purposes. Also, in many opera houses, nested other recording devices which were *sneaked* in, *bribed* in, but certainly not *invited* in; their issue ultimately found the way into a small, but passionate, market as *pirates* whose sound quality, with a very few exceptions, approximates aural torture. Yet, even the worst of these do I now regard nostalgically as I hear a faint knock at the door– it's *Ampie the Alien*, surely not of my world.

---

*This term refers to baritones who possess sufficient volume and timbre to successfully perform the dramatic arias in Verdi operas such as *Aida*, *Rigoletto* and the like.

In the last decade of the last century, and wrapped with the benign insulation of *sound enhancement*, the *amplification* microphone entered the opera house and the last main bastion of the vocal fortress was finally breached. That wonderful demi-god, the glorious *stentor*, whose only assistance came from the divine, was now being offered *enhancement* (say, friend, is that frog still in there?) It was generally known that the smaller scaled *Broadway* voice occasionally begged a hand in this fashion, but why the opera singer who never needed it before? Because, in this same time frame, the *Broadway* voice and that in *opera* became far more similar in sound, so what harm could a little electrical boost do? (Excuse me, would you take a quick peek and see if that frog is still moving?)

What *crept* into the opera house *leapt* into the recording studio. Early in the 1980's, the birth of *digital* recording marked the 35-year-old *analog* LP for extinction*.

Caruso, who surely required several retakes in 1902 but didn't get any, once noted that errors in the opera house would be remembered by a very few for a little while but a recorded flaw would be eternal. A century later, there would be no need for fear as that eternity would no longer threaten. From its inception around the turn of the 20th century through the 1970's, the proclaimed quest of recorded opera was to most closely approximate the original source, the *live* experience, this becoming

---

*For over a century following Edison's 1877 *Phonograph*, sound waves were recorded and reproduced in a fashion parallel or *analogous* (thus ANALOG) to the original source. Around 1980, a new system now stored the waves in precise *numerical* (thus DIGITAL) units with much better fidelity and no degradation via playback: this also allowed virtually infinite possibilities for deletion, alteration and replacement of imperfections.

far more realistically attainable with the advent of the electric microphone around 1925. But now, a new technology stimulated a new thinking which created a new reality: live humans possess *imperfections* which, when manifested, should be eliminated prior to the release of the final product. I am not referring here to *retakes* which have always been time consuming, costly and generally discouraged. It would, however, be misleading, as well as dishonest, to imply that *adjustment assistance* was foreign to recording in the pre-digital age.

Around 1950, and well past her prime years, the wildly popular *leggiera* (light) soprano Lily Pons *cracked* on a high note during a live performance of Donizetti's *Lucia di Lammermoor*. The Met had *an angel on its shoulder* as that performance was to be delay-broadcast the next day when, at the fateful spot, an accurately clear note was heard which was *borrowed* from the singer's earlier Columbia recording of the opera. And, a bit later, RCA Victor performed *deep therapeutic massage* in *adjusting* some very uneven takes of the aging dramatic soprano Zinka Milanov.

What modern digital technology has done is to elevate sonic prestidigitation to the level of a fine art. In the July/August 1996 issue of *Stereo Review*, J.A. Van Sant, in "Sounding Off: When Hearing Is Not Believing," directly addressed the issue of alteration. Van Sant focused most closely on a Sony recording of Verdi's *Il Trovatore* which was "...in process..." for three years so that pitch adjustments and related changes could be properly effected. Additionally, a ringing high 'C' emanated from Domingo's throat at the conclusion of "Di Quella Pira" ("From that Pyre"), no matter that the durable fine tenor effectively lacked that note and really offered a 'B' (what a difference that small semi-tone makes).
Van Sant summarized:

> "Quite some of what we ultimately heard on that recording represents the achievement of present-day digital technology, reworking and recreating sound, bionic sound— part real, part fake, ..." and concluded by pondering the concept of "...ethics in recording and broadcasting...?" Ethics!

Let me offer a somewhat analogous personal example. After recently recording a new *promo* for *The Joy of Opera* and gratified that I was able to get through the 50 seconds without error, I was a bit surprised when the recording engineer said he wanted to delete something and asked, during the playback, if I knew what it was? Truly, I didn't have a clue. What was soon to be eliminated was a scarcely audible inhalation – whoa, I breathed a bit– as I then watched a pulsating *Doppler*-like color line zero in on a given spot and, ZAP, I was rendered *breathless* between two words.

One final non-operatic statement is eminently worthy of inclusion here. Speaking of the current pop music scene, Al Bell (record company owner and former Motown president) covered similar ground in discussing the current capabilities of high-tech recording equipment:

> "What I've seen it do is allow a person with mediocre talent to excel because of the technology, and maintain that mediocrity..."*

Bell continued with respect to *lip-synching* and *quick takes*, where the *technician* almost becomes the *musician*. He looked back wistfully to the *good old days* in the *pop* studio when sometimes 40-50 takes were made in the attempt to "...capture the magic." In the *good old days* at the opera house, only one *unassisted shot* was allowed for such capture. So now, yet again, but for the last time, "Nuff said!"

I believe I coined a catchy, but relevant, little phrase in describing the 3 step method of *sanitization* which incorporates a new 3 R's:

NIX - (Rejection of any actual or perceived flaw)
MIX - (Readjusting, or reworking, that flaw)
FIX - (Replacement of the original offender)

*Reprinted in the *Florida Times Union*, July 11, 2004.

It is highly unlikely that what you are now listening to, on that shiny 4½ inch plastic wafer known as the *Compact Disc*, is an accurate representation of what originally occurred. Alas, *opera* is no exception in what increasingly tends to evolve into a virtually undetectable, yet vaguely perceived, *predictable perfection*.

"What errors do you want obliterated?" asked the sound engineer of his boss just before "as many as we can find" returned from the other side of the glass.

Welcome to the brave new world of *opera* and, as it's the only one we have around here now, let's at least *try* to make it as THRILLING as we can.

13 - Defusing the Land Mines (Reprise)

If I truly felt the future of *opera* to be archaic, I would have opted to compose variations on "Thanks for the Memory"* rather than embark on this effort. Truth be told, however, the magnificent 400 year old *experiment* is currently drifting towards particularly turbulent waters and an objective analysis, with viable strategies, is very much in order to, at least, maintain some level of relevance in 21st century America.

Up to now, emphasis has been given to the two forces which *repel*, rather than *entice*, a wider and younger following. Both as reminder and warning, let us now summarize this pair of *turn-offs*:

♪ *Opera's* association with a vitally necessary but artificial group of *stuffshirts* with skyward pointed noses under which the *clink* of the colliding crystal champagne glasses approximates the *squillo* of a Roberta Peters high 'F' (Chapter 5) **and**,

♪ A non-litigatable form of child abuse by which otherwise responsible adults allow, and even encourage, a catastrophic trauma to the ears, *Eustachian*** tubes and tympanic membranes of their offspring, invariably resulting in permanent revulsion towards *opera* (Chapter 6).

The remainder of this work focuses on current realities of enormous consequence which directly impacts, and transcends, the art form itself, dealing rather with the fundamental shifting of the American cultural aesthetic. Change, that only true constant, often tends to come with some graduality and, at times, has been scarcely perceptible at all.

---

*Almost everyone hears the line as "Thanks for the *Memories*" but the song pays homage to the various *individual* remembrances in the singular.
**Named for the Italian anatomist Bartolommeo Eustachio (1524?-74)— <u>Note</u>: he died just before the birth of *opera*. Is there deeper meaning here?

The second half of the 20th century would not be one of those times, most dramatically not. In one of the most condensed upheavals on record, the art form *opera* would not get the protection of higher ground as the terrain was inherently altered: ultimate damage assessment is still being evaluated.

With this said, this book was written not as a eulogy, but an appraisal commissioned by concern. Of import here is to realize that *opera* in the U.S. is not, and has never been, government financed as is the case in Europe, its birthplace. If it is to continue in functioning relevance, an inexorable force must be addressed without delay as neglect may well relegate the most profoundly moving art form ever created by humans to its own *gilded box* in that highly overcrowded *dustbin of history.*

As stated, I intend to end this work on a note of realistic, but limited, optimism with pragmatic suggestions as to how to push that great *hodgepodge of the Renaissance* onwards and upwards, though decidedly upwards to be sure. The road ahead is neither smooth nor welcoming: to pretend otherwise, as we reconnoiter the altered landscape, would be as evasively dishonest as it would be irrelevantly academic.

With the aforementioned crystal champagne glasses, let us propose a *toast* and *clink and drink* to an operatic future!

14 - An Uphill Journey

There was a *lotta lookin* in the first half of the 16th century as the *new world* conjured an anxious wonder and the vessels of the French, Spanish, and English initially kept a comfortable distance. From the shore side, the natives of countless millennia cast a cautious eye seaward. When the gazing finally yielded to landing, a Spanish chronicler– and, undoubtedly, that SW European country's leading music critic– noted "...sounds of *horror* rather than *harmony*..." when he heard the *orchestration* of the Paleo-Indians on the west coast of the peninsula already named *Pasqua Florida* (Easter flowers) by Juan Ponce de León in that century's second decade. As with all primitive societies, the Spaniard encountered the primacy of *rhythm* over the *harmony* of his homeland. What he certainly did not hear was *opera* which would not see birth, and not very far from that homeland, for another six decades. Surely the first *harmony* heard here was "Te Deum Laudamus" (We Praise Thee Lord), which was always sung after successful sea journeys. But the *new world* would greatly disappoint here as there was no gold nor silver nor eternal youth via flowing fountain.

17th century pre-U.S.A. saw the Spanish continue in St. Augustine to the background musical accompaniment of the *vihuela* (from the same root as *violin*), the forerunner of the modern Spanish classical guitar. The English Colonists in Jamestown, VA in 1607 were later joined by their New England brethren and their *flutes 'n lutes*. And, in early *big apple land* it was Niew Amsterdam as the Dutch imprinted their mark.

When our founders declared independence, *opera* was closing out its second century and began to sprout wings in our nascent nation. Though never conclusively authenticated, it is believed that the initial American performance of Gluck's seminal masterpiece *Orfeo ed Euridice* was given in Charleston, SC in 1794. There is little doubt that major European operas were performed in the original thirteen in the 18th century.

A bit of perspective at this point should serve to re-calibrate our operatic compass. At the time of our Constitutional Convention, Mozart would live only four more years, Beethoven was a highly promising teenager and Verdi and Wagner, opera's titans, would not be born for another two and one-half decades in another century, opera's most glorious century.

Though Florida had been French and Spanish, the rest of the fledgling United States was overwhelmingly Anglo-Saxon and Scotch-Irish. And, then, there was New Orleans. The Louisiana Purchase of 1803 tripled the area of this country in one fell swoop. The once French settlement port city at the mouth of the Mississippi River was the true cultural melting pot for both Negroes and Caucasians in the early 19th century, boasting more opera companies and concert halls than any other city in America. The diverse flavors of Europe (France, Spain, Italy, Germany, England, Scotland and Ireland) could be readily heard in the songs of the city named for the Duke of Orleans.

As the 19th century matured, the major cities proudly displayed their gilded new opera houses where repertories tended to reflect populations. At the gigantic new 4,000 seat Metropolitan Opera House in New York City which opened in 1883, the works were predominately German as were the investors and boardroom. Within just one generation, however, this would change as emigration shifted to Italy and Eastern Europe at the turn of the 20th century. Spain, however, never embraced *opera* in the same way because of its vibrantly unique ancestry of Arab, Moor, Sephardic Jew, and Gypsy. Additionally, that polyglot population fancied a sprightly *operetta* style known as *Zarzuela*, named for the theater where it was first performed. Spain's non-*opera* essence will take on enormous importance and shall be discussed in proper context in this work's penultimate chapter.

When the great European migration finally began to wane in the early 20th century, the splendid public school system in virtually every heavily populated American city reflected the tastes and cultures of the new residents and, playing a most vital role, was the curriculum area generally labeled *Music Appreciation*.

Even while weathering the most ominous storms of the two World Wars, the foundation of this educational segment for the new first generation citizens appeared unshakable in perpetuity.

Taken for granted then, but surprising in retrospect, almost all my friends in my Brooklyn of the 1940's had a respect for, and a basic knowledge of, classical music and opera, yet few sprouted from musical homes such as mine. What enabled this to so succeed was the two-parent support of the passionately dedicated music teachers, a major part of elementary education. Such a gem was Mrs. Heinlein, more of whom a bit later. And, so providentially convergent, there was *radio*.

Ted Buchter, the *Lighting Director's Son* of Chapter 11, recently related a vivid childhood memory. In his elementary school in the mid-1930's, NBC's very popular *Music Appreciation Hour* was *piped in* to the classroom and a homework assignment was given for return the following week. That program, which aired from 1927-47, was directed by Walter Damrosch (1862-1950) who conducted the first symphonic broadcast with the New York Symphony Society (founded by his father Leopold) in 1925. Children nationwide were exposed to this program with permanent life enriching results. Damrosch also created *catchy* rhymes, to go with the main themes which aided greatly the musical digestion of many for a very long time – a vivid illustration follows shortly. First, however, I believe that a vest pocket bio of arguably the most significant father and son team of instrumental and opera music in U.S. history is in order.

Leopold Damrosch, Selesian (Polish) by birth, initially studied medicine but yielded to the call of his primary passion, *music*. He became Director and Conductor of the Metropolitan Opera Association in its second season (1884-85) and immediately turned a deficit into a profit through a daring move of presenting all operas– including such Italian standards as *Aida*– in German, clearly realizing that the large late 19th century German population in the increasingly prestigious metropolis would support this decision. Acting as *impresario* as well, and probably overtaxing his resistance, the elder Damrosch contracted pneumonia and died shortly after his first opening night.

Walter, only 23 at the time, assumed his father's duties as conductor to mixed reviews but it would not, however, be those performances from which Damrosch the Younger would leave his indelible mark on the early 20th century American music scene. Radio changed everything at the end of the first quarter of the 20th century as veritable *new worlds* entered homes through that *wonderbox*. Gone was the "...infernal funnel" (Caruso's description), the cumbersome acoustic horn which *swallowed* many a fine voice and reputation. The old Victor Talking Machine Company was now RCA Victor after merging with the Radio Corporation of America in 1927 and "Nipper," wondrously listening to *his master's voice*, would remain, horn and all. But it would now be the electric microphone which could not only record but broadcast live– LIVE! And, yet again, a Damrosch was at the helm in a voyage into history.

So, indeed, into Ted's classroom came the magical NBC broadcast as the lighting director illuminated the old Met in his 25th year and his wife, retired from the *corps de ballet* there, probably wondered why she didn't retain those sketches presented to her by *The Great Caruso* so many years earlier. And, though he may not have realized it at the time, young Ted was immersed in *opera* in a most special way. When a decade later, I followed Ted to that point in elementary education in New York City, I didn't get Mr. Damrosch but his devoted disciple, Mrs. Heinlein. Using *gramophone* records (oops! I almost wrote *phonograph*), she discussed and analyzed, at the level of her students, the music with a living vibrancy. Her use of the *Damrosch Ditties* made a lifelong impression. Here is a particularly indelible example where, to the *swaying* 'ebb and *flow*' of the mesmerizing melody, we added in soft *staccato*:

♪ - ♪ - ♪ - ♪ - ♪ - ♪ - ♪ - ♪ - ♪ - ♪ - ♪ - ♪ - ♪ - ♪ - ♪

BAR-CAR-ROLL,
FROM-TAY-YELLS OF HOFF-MON,
WRIT-TEN BY OFF-IN-BOCK!

♪ - ♪ - ♪ - ♪ - ♪ - ♪ - ♪ - ♪ - ♪ - ♪ - ♪ - ♪ - ♪ - ♪ - ♪

Unforgettable, literally, is the proper word to describe this method of instruction.

The music Ted and I heard in our schools in the 1930's and 1940's followed the original road of *opera*: Italy, Germany, France, England, Russia, a quick taste of Spain via deFalla and Scandinavia, complements of Grieg and Sibelius. And where were our native composers? Oh, there were a few: Louis Moreau Gottschalk (1829-69) of New Orleans, child prodigy whose music, over time, fell out of fashion and Stephen Collins Foster (1826-64) who achieved phenomenal popularity with his infectious *folk-like* melodies which are currently, yet probably only temporarily, asynchronous with contemporary fashion. Then there was Edward MacDowell* (1860-1908) who, though born in New York City, was thoroughly European in study, style and personality. Composing mainly for the piano, MacDowell wrote virtually nothing for voice.

At the turn of the 20th century, the closest thing to the first true *American* opera was composed by Frederick Delius (1862-1934) who spent some time in North Florida in the early 1880's, stamping a profound impression on his subsequent musical mentality. Delius, however, was born in England so the wonderful story of *Koanga* (1904), the proud African Prince forced to work on an18th century New Orleans plantation, and his love, betrayal, violent death and vengeance, does not qualify on the grounds of the composer's birthplace.

Scott Joplin (1868-1917), the *Ragtime King*, thankfully rescued from obscurity by that fine film *The Sting*, wrote *Treemonisha*, an opera that has remained elusive despite several successful productions and some highly interesting musical ideas which, regrettably, do not consistently run through the work's structure.

Although *American opera*– written by Americans– existed since the last years of the 18th century, very few were ever warmly embraced by the general public. Some received immediate critical acclaim but, as audiences desired no repetition, they quickly withered on the musical vine.

*What piano student, in earlier times, did not have to study "To a Wild Rose" from *Woodland Sketches* (1896)?

Occasionally, a truly unique personality transcended a work which then faded with the singer, as was the case with Lawrence Tibbett's sensational portrayal of Louis Gruenberg's* *The Emperor Jones* (based on Eugene O'Neill) at the Metropolitan Opera in 1933. Emphasis, then, is placed on lasting public favor, or lack thereof, rather than elitist critical accolades where the works praised frequently faded before the ink dried. This is, unfortunately, also the case with the two operas of Aaron Copland (1900-1990), arguably America's greatest composer. *The Tender Land* (1954), his best, is a most interesting work in many ways but has remained obscure even to those who possess more than a modicum of operatic savvy.

Lasting posterity would come with two composers born around the turn of the 20th century in New York City: Jerome Kern (1885-1945) and George Gershwin (1898-1937), the *pathfinders* who firmly placed the term *American opera* on the melodic map. Was that one or both eyebrows you just raised at my linkage of Kern and opera? Allow me to present a supportive position.

As backdrop, a bit of quick retro-perspective: Giacomo Puccini (1858-1924) died before completing his last opera *Turandot* which premiered, after completion by composer Franco Alfano (with Toscanini's supervision), in 1926. *Turandot* would prove to be the last standard repertory opera, mainly due to incomparable performances with Nilsson and Corelli in the late 1950s and early 60s.

The very next year (1927), Kern and Hammerstein's *Show Boat* opened in New York City and it transformed the existing landscape on Broadway. Coming at a time when popular acceptance of its theme might have been impossible were it not for the unchallenged reputations of composer and librettist, it dealt directly and eloquently with social and racial sensitivities when the contemporary *revues de jour* parodied and stereotyped them. This departure of courageous magnitude also *yanked* offstage, via the *bo-peep* burlesque hook, the *vaudevillian patchworks* where musical and literary cohesion was neither sought nor received.

---

* Gruenberg was born in Poland, but came to the United States at the age of two.

Achieving powerful fidelity to the Edna Ferber original, *Show Boat* was profoundly innovative and may well have fostered a rethinking in its adoring audiences. Music and lyrics, for the first time in this genre, achieved meaningful unity. "Ol' Man River" ("I'm tired of livin' and scared of dyin'") is worthy of Verdi. Capt. Andy Hawks, seeking to keep *dirty laundry* hidden, keeps reminding us of the "...one big haapppy family" on the Cotton Blossom while the emotional pain is almost palpable. Julie, assumed Caucasian, offers a poignantly subtle mixture of American *blues* and *jazz* (only about a decade old when *Show Boat* bowed) with "Bill" and "Can't Help Lovin' Dat Man," the latter surprising Queenie who heard only "...colored people sing that song." "You Are Love" is "O Soave Fanciulla"* on the Mississippi. *Show Boat* also requires, at a minimum, voices of resonant caliber and the work has properly entered the repertories of several companies since the New York City Opera first summoned it in 1954. And, as the *great experiment* will soon dip itself into *crossover* (Chapter 15 and Epilogue), *Show Boat* will even begin to sound positively Wagnerian.

Of greatest importance are the contributions of Oscar Hammerstein II, a *librettist* of the old school rather than a *lyricist* of the new. Coming from operatic soil– grandfather Oscar almost put the Metropolitan Opera out of business at the turn of the 20th century– his verse almost *impels* the composer to place specific notes in specific ways. A graphic example occurs in the Kern-Hammerstein song "The Folks Who Live on the Hill" from the 1937 MGM picture *High, Wide and Handsome*. In describing the wonderful family, land and house, the singer extols:

> "Our ver**AN**dah will comm**AN**d - a view of meadows green..."

Any of you who are familiar with the song should heartily agree that the *float* of that line almost composes itself. Kern, upon reading it, must have thanked his lucky stars for having had Hammerstein.

---

*"O Sweet Maiden," the duet which ends Act I of *La Bohème*. With some frustration, I continue to fail in my attempt to establish Kern's familiarity with, and adulation of, Giacomo Puccini.

But *Show Boat* an opera? Admittedly, Kern did need help in beefing up his slender orchestration and received it in Robert Russell Bennett. Spoken dialogue? Nothing new here as *The Magic Flute* and *Carmen* (Singspiel and Opera Comique respectively: see Glossary) attest. Somewhat lighter opera? Sure, but certainly not *operetta* or *musical comedy* although effective homage is paid to the fading *vaudeville* in "Life Upon the Wicked Stage" and "I Might Fall Back On You."

Yet, when considered in the context of that time and place, it too serves to intensify the drama as one realizes that the 19th century was nostalgically yielding as "After The Ball Is Over" was sung by all on New Year's Eve in the year 1900.*

An old critical analysis of *Show Boat* debated Kern's title of *father* of the American musical (their word, not mine). To paraphrase and update, Kern surely would have been ordered to donate DNA to conclusively verify that paternity. *Show Boat* did to Broadway in the early 20th century what *opera* did in Florence in the last years of the 16th: offering the *folks* something wonderfully innovative that they would embrace and adore.

Kern, of course, would also pass the torch, as well as the magnificent Hammerstein, to his admiring younger contemporary Richard Rodgers who would push that genre on from the middle of World War II to the *Rock*, as opposed to the *Stone*, Age.

The *bible* of comprehensive opera books, *The World of Opera* (Appendix D), includes no mention either of *Show Boat* or its creator, as the authors patently dismiss it as *opera* and they are far from alone in this view. Begging to differ, with the very highest degree of respect, is "Opera's Regular Guy" who once closed a *Joy of Opera* program with the words "...this was one man's opinion, MINE!" And, I do believe, I am not alone either. So, within that context, *Show Boat* is decidedly American and *American opera* just when we needed it.

*With the title "After the Ball," this 1892 song by Charles K. Harris, was the first million copy *hit* in the *pop* tune field. In most productions of *Show Boat*, it is *borrowed*.

Porgy and Bess followed Show Boat eight years later. Based on DuBose Heyward's Porgy, Gershwin strayed from his comfort zone of the stage musical with particularly evocative and, in many ways, innovative results. Despite sporadic lapses in the work, the composer has pulled the gold ring of public acceptance across oceans. No American opera has ever been more accepted internationally while many more scholarly efforts have long since receded into oblivion.

And, not to be outdone, The Opera Reader makes no mention whatever of this work or its composer. "Chàcun a son gout."*

You know the feeling you sometimes get when things seem just a little too comfortable, a bit too easy? Such a time was the 1950's. When TV augmented radio, it portended enormous promise for opera. Not only would we hear, and now see, the greatest of singers on The Voice of Firestone (NBC 1949-54 and ABC 1954-63) and The Bell Telephone Hour (CBS 1959-68) but smaller opera company productions were telecast, one hosted by the venerable tenor Giovanni Martinelli. Leontyne Price, the Bess of Gershwin's dreams, was Tosca in a very early NBC production of the work in 1955. And, of paramount importance, the unbelievably popular Ed Sullivan Show** was particularly opera friendly. Act II of Tosca with Maria Callas and George London was a major event and even such esoteric European legends as the great WW II vintage baritone Gino Bechi appeared on Sullivan's stage. Opera was everywhere. Glory, hallelujah!! It was much the same with early live TV stage drama in programs such as Studio One and Playhouse 90, where many a screen career blossomed (Charlton Heston, Eva Marie Saint, and Paul Newman come to immediate mind).

---

*"Each to his taste" or "To each his own." In J. Strauss' incomparable operetta Die Fledermaus, Prince Orlofsky sings of this in a wonderful aria. Operetta is an art form all its own although it is not included in the focus of this primer.
**Called Toast of the Town from 1948-55, this program was the longest running variety show which aired 23 years when it left in 1971 with virtually no opera.

And, back to *opera*, it seemed that a universal *golden age* was at hand as that small black and white TV tube, in the huge cabinet, would now enhance radio which, in turn, so superbly supported the sainted music teachers of the melodic classroom. It also must be emphasized that these *opera* related programs were telecast on the *commercial* networks as *popular entertainment*.

A retrospective analysis of *The Ed Sullivan* Show* can provide a fascinating historical snapshot of the changing American entertainment culture in the mid-portion of the 20th century. The early viewers– 1948 through the 50's– were typically grandparents from Europe, their first generation American born children, and *their* offspring, the first of the *boomers* born shortly after the Second World War. Dispersed around a myriad group of magicians, jugglers, acrobats and ventriloquists were the great opera singers of the day. As we settled in, a little later, to see and hear more of those glorious voices, *Topo Gigio* and *Seňor Wences* came of age.

In discernable contrast were the shows of the end years. Most of the elders of the *old world* were gone now and, as the American born adult *children* busied themselves with other things, their own now bobbed wildly back and forth to *Rock n' Roll*, the *craze* that *surely couldn't last.* But where was *opera* now a dwindling few may have wondered? *Opera*? As some of us used to say in Brooklyn, "never 'hoid' of 'im."

Yes, the *nirvana* of those early shows would vanish in a mere blink of the CBS eye. What was about to happen has occurred for all of human history, the inevitable yielding of one moment in time to the next. But this differed in the sheer speed of the changeover from the first full postwar decade to the 1960's, when the *'a changin' times'* sung of by Bob Dylan came fast and furious.

*My paternal grandmother pronounced the name "Red Solomon"

The new wave eroded the existing shorelines: *The Bell Telephone Hour* and *The Voice of Firestone* would not survive the 60's. Ed Sullivan reduced, and then rather eliminated, *opera* from the show's format as the *new music* proliferated.*

Something else was also happening, imperceptibly at first, which would, more than any other single factor, place a barrier between *opera* and the elementary school youth of the 1960's. *Music Appreciation*, and the parental support that nourished it, was disappearing from the public schools. Tight budgets were nothing new and the *dexterous dollar juggling act* was always performed, but *Music Appreciation* somehow remained immune and invulnerable until the 1950's. Symbolically, Walter Damrosch, who was also Music Adviser to the New York City Board of Education, died in 1950 as the shadow of the cost trimming blade began to be seen in the classrooms where European music was now more faintly heard as the small oak chairs, with the right hand desk arms, were now being filled by children of non-European heritage.

And, of enormous impact, television, born in the 1940's and blossoming in the 50's, began to assume a surrogate role, *parenting*. The culture was no longer being passed through *generations* but through the *tube*, from *tradition* to *transmission*. It became apparent that the market could now target the youth directly as their dazed parents lingered rather motionless in the background. The age of *anything goes* was at hand when it was realized that virtually anything would *sell* if effectively marketed to this highly impressionable young group of consumers. What clearly was no longer being offered for sale was classical music and opera.

The changing TV culture in the ensuing decades would command much greater power when, as some called it *progress*, two jobs were needed where one sufficed before and both parents worked outside the home where only one did previously.

---

*With the *one-two punch* of Elvis Presley in the late 50's and the historic appearance of The Beatles in 1964, the Sullivan Show immediately shifted the focus directly toward the new teenage *boomers*, who were toddlers when the program began.

"You're on your own kid- Granma's in the nursing home now- be good- food in fridge- watch TV, see ya later."

                                        Love, M & D

As "what is music?" and "what is art?," "whose music?" and "whose art?" were being debated while Music and Art were being diluted, the marketing gurus were beginning to salivate.

15 - Steering Away from a Dead-End Street

"...freakishness masquerading as creativity."
–Alistair Cooke

Cautiously venturing from the sanctity of the Roman Church at first, as did its founding genius Monteverdi, *opera* soon sprouted from its rich Renaissance soil, fertilized by fervor and passion, and spread throughout Europe like wildflowers. It went its way with an existing roadmap, the harmony* of that Mother Church. No formal system of horizontal line musical notation existed before the 11th century. The Ancient Greeks used a lettering system to place the relationship of tones and, later, medieval scribes employed an array of *slashes*– called *neumes*– so one could distinguish ascending from descending tones. So, when Monteverdi came of age as the 17th century dawned, the *universal* system was accepted for over a half millennium. Instrumental and harmonic evolution through the ensuing two centuries remained consonantly friendly to post-Renaissance European ears until Beethoven (1770-1827), when enduring an agonizing loss of hearing, that tormented titan shattered virtually all existing boundaries and, unwittingly, reconfigured the entire musical landscape. As a result, experimentation and alteration began not long after the death of music's most influential giant who, rather than simply being ahead of *his* time, transcended time itself.

As we have seen, when *opera* was imported to America, it found receptive European ears in eager anticipation. This was not surprising since, at the time of the birth of our Republic when the voluntarily arriving population of the United States was less than four million, natives of the British Isles and Germany predominated. Exceptions concerned Florida (St. Augustine) which, until 1821, was under a Spanish flag for a second time, and the unique New Orleans tightly held its fascinating French heritage.

---

*A specific system of chords (three or more notes sounded simultaneously) which was accepted throughout Europe since the Middle Ages.

When the first shot was heard at Fort Sumter, the nation's *movers and shakers* were overwhelmingly Anglo-Saxon and Scotch-Irish. It would, however, not be from these roots that our one true domestic musical form would derive and it would emphatically not, at least initially, be *opera*. In our blessed mainland, lying between this planet's two vastest oceans, it would spring from our African-born residents who most certainly did not come here willingly. It would meander through their Florida-born *cakewalks* and New Orleans-bred *ragged rhythms* which would merge with the old and reworked lament-chants termed *blues*. And it would wear, and ultimately with pride, the vulgar appellation (given it by others) *jizz*, then *jass* and finally *jazz*, while offering up this land's only homegrown original music, blossoming in the second decade of the last century on military instruments only becoming affordable to them after the indelible War between the States. But since this form is non-operatic, we shall take our leave as it is now deservedly and extensively covered elsewhere in descriptive musical analysis.

After World War II, a dramatic shift in immigration tilted away from Europe and toward Latin-America and Asia and, since 1950, aided by the advent of jet travel, the influx of Latinos, Africans and Asians rose to a level not seen since the pre-World War I days. The historical peak of all U.S. immigration was from 1900 to 1910 when over eight million Europeans landed on these shores, but this summit may well be scaled in the near future.

In overview, then, the demographic trend of international migration to the U.S. veered away from Western and Eastern Europe toward Asia, Africa and various Spanish speaking countries and this direction appears to be firmly focused for the foreseeable future.

In starkest contrast to the U.S. mainland, the end of the Second World War saw much of Europe in shambles. In 1946, the bomb-damaged La Scala Opera House in Milan was reconstructed and the octogenarian conducting legend Arturo Toscanini proclaimed the house *fit* with a single clap of his hands and music again reverberated in that venerable shrine. In the cast was the youthful Renata Tebaldi who Toscanini described as possessing "la voce d'angelo"– the voice of an angel– and vocal history would lovingly agree.

Opera, live and recorded, was back big time on both sides of the Atlantic, the long playing 33⅓ rpm vinyl record was here and the *days of glory* were ours.

During the dark war years at the Metropolitan Opera, the helm was manned by a former singer, Canadian-born Edward Johnson. Like Beethoven's *Fourth Symphony*, the passing years have all but obscured his tenure between the imposing pillars of Gatti-Casazza before him and Bing who would follow. As in World War I, the great European artists would not risk an ocean crossing and, as a result, Johnson harvested his considerable American talent which would proliferate gloriously in Bing's regime. With the gradual return of the great European singers after the War, the 1950's can be regarded as the richest golden age in the history of the Metropolitan Opera.

Yes, for many of us who were young then, these years are retrospectively regarded with the fondest nostalgia. This is particularly true in matters operatic where we were treated to the sounds of the greatest array of American vocal talent imaginable, those first generation titans who, with few exceptions, were the children of immigrants. Their magnificence rendered the need for European stars far less mandatory: WE, in splendor, have indeed arrived!

As immigration resurged, the untouched U.S. mainland again became the most desirable place on Earth but, this time, it would not be the Great Statue's Torch which would light the way at the end of a weary Westward journey.

The bottom line is indelibly clear: domestic opera companies best not ignore the shift in U.S. population over the last half century. As focused on in the Epilogue, *flexibility* and *measured experimentation* will be absolute prerequisites for survival and two main reasons stand out. First, the underwriting *opera goer* (Chapter 5), without whom the fledgling would never have taken wing in the first place, is aging and no longer being replaced automatically from a long waiting line of eager young elegant aspirants. And, as previously discussed, the standard repertory has lost much of its drawing magnetism, made far more problematical by the scarcity of the great big thrilling voices in all categories (Chapter 12). With the overall backdrop of the immigration shift *away* from opera rooted lands, any administration which chooses to cater only to the past will simultaneously be committing fiscal suicide. And, as noted at the end of Chapter 13, that *toast* will then BE *toast*, as the art form and it's "Igarrophant" will be viewed by future eyes as museum relics.

As this nascent century proceeds, one may safely wager in the prediction that the settings and sounds from theaters will increasingly reflect *Opera Latino-Americanismo*. According to the U.S. Census Bureau's projections (released early in 2004), the nation's Hispanic population will increase 188% by 2050, up from 35.6 million to 102.6 million or about a full one-third of the total population in this country. And belatedly, as done with *Show Boat*, the doors of many opera houses will swing open to *West Side Story* and as yet unborn kindred creations.

In my opinion, the only viable road open to opera companies in these earliest years of the new century is to honestly explore and carefully consider *crossover* where the possibilities are endless both in terms of *milieu* (oops, setting that is) and the very nature of musical format as traditionally defined. It is, however, in this *crossing* itself where the double-edged sword begins to swing and, without a shadow of a doubt, *opera's* future hangs in the balance, for there is quicksand galore in this land of *Anything Goes*, even though it will surely be renamed *Imaginative Innovation*.

Consider this: in 1951, recordings like "Be My Love" with Mario Lanza and Tony Bennett's "Just Say I Love Her" (from the Italian song "Dicitencello vuie!") made the *pop Hit Parade* (how operatic, in retro, they now sound). By contrast, 50 years later, ALL of Billboard's 'Top 10' of 2003 were *Rap* and *Hip-Hop*, giving *recitative* a dramatic new meaning.

Perhaps, then, as this primer now approaches its conclusion, a few more of you will agree with me that *Show Boat* is indeed *opera*.   Strange, how sweetly, yet irrelevantly, academic that discussion seems now as the future will care little of nostalgic indulgence, so the matter of what constitutes *operatic cuisine*, and its attendant spices and seasonings, will now have to be placed on the melodic back burner as your THREE COURSE...

16 - "… Dinner is Served"

FIRST COURSE:	The "Regular Guy" Rx for Instant Opera Enhancement: *(Guaranteed Benefits-No Side Effects)*

Any success ultimately achieved by this primer, even allowing for some aversion caused by the entities discussed in Chapters 5 and 6, assumes one key ingredient: a surviving open mind. Your author does not pre-suppose, in the reader, any measurable degree of knowledge or familiarity with the unique art form curiously called *opera*. Accordingly, no needlessly complex publications will be recommended here and elsewhere in this effort. I will, however, list in the Basic Bibliography (Appendix D) several enduring classics of the genre, viewed within the context of an ultimate goal post in a long distance drive after short, but consistent, gains.

Goldilocks and The Three Bears came to mind in a quick re-scanning of the operatic literature of my golden era, the 1950's and early 60's. Regarding the essential stories of the most popular operas, Milton J. Cross' *Complete Stories of the Great Operas* devotes over 600 pages in offering highly detailed act-by-act narratives of 72 works. Conversely, *The Opera Reader* (edited by Louis Biancolli), though it was not that work's sole purpose, offered a scant few paragraphs to the same, while covering 90 operas, many long gone from the repertories of the vast majority of international opera shrines.

So, then, what is *too much*, *too little* and, most elusive, *just right*?

♪ - ♪ - ♪ - ♪ - ♪ - ♪ - ♪ - ♪ - ♪ - ♪ - ♪ - ♪ - ♪ - ♪ - ♪ - ♪ - ♪

In the *Prelude* of this book, I noted that *Opera: You Never Knew You Loved It* is offered as "...a palatable appetizer which should much enhance the cuisine to follow." Though a few highly selected *gourmet delights* for the "...more sumptuous dining..." are listed, as previously stated, the focus is clearly at the starting gate, before any hurdles come into view, let alone loom directly in front of us. It is much easier to progress in stages than it is to abruptly reverse course and then attempt to recover. Let's begin, then, with a simple, but vital, sequence under the vanishing banner proclaiming "Less is Best"!

> **STEP 1**- Read the stories of the standard operas, preferably in the order recommended:
>> **Basic Level**- Thomas Matthews, *Stories of the World's Great Operas*, Golden Press, 1968 (used bookstores are great sources for out-of-print items).
>> **Intermediate Level**- Henry W. Simon, *100 Great Operas and Their Stories*, Anchor Books, 1989.

(IMPORTANT: If *opera* is essentially a new experience, do not listen to any music at this point.)

> **STEP 2**- Obtain CD's, as suggested, with enclosed *librettos* (unless already available), giving side-by-side translations from the language of the opera into English.* I highly recommend *complete* operas rather than *highlights* unless otherwise stated. R. Strauss' *Der Rosenkavalier* (requiring three CD's) is one example where excerpts are suggested, as the *flow* of the magical *appetizers* of this unique work should be digested before the somewhat complex main course is served. Read the background information (if offered) and peruse the *libretto* (still no music while you'll derive a good feel of the *flow* of the stage action). Taking your time here will shortly pay dividends.

---

*In the **analog** LP era (roughly pre-1982), *librettos* measured 12"x12" and were very friendly to the eyes. By contrast, their CD counterparts (5"x5") frequently require magnification even from pre-Medicare *folk*.

STEP 3- Allow sufficient time, relax and listen to the entire opera using the *libretto* as a guide, if needed, but don't let it distract too much from the music and singing. The main ingredient here is to **feel** what you are experiencing. Breaking up the effort by listening to individual segments at different times tends to interrupt the *momentum of flow* which is so important in the unique *gestalt* that is *opera*.

STEP 4- Consider renting/purchasing modern opera videos on VHS or DVD in the suggested order. These videos are vocally, scenically, and dramatically cohesive and are aided by unobtrusive, properly timed *sub* or *super* titles. Many are *shot* outdoors in lavish productions, far beyond the means of any opera house, under the experienced guidance of world-class film directors such as Franco Zeffirelli. Again, relish these videos without interruption.

STEP 5- Bask in the glow and passion that is *opera* at its best. If the first signs of *opera addiction* appear, call for help at susbrody@aol.com.

ALTERNATE SEQUENCE- Owing to the differences in human beings, a variant of the above is suggested for those of you who are more visual than audile. Hence (I've always liked the resolute sound of that Old English derivative), STEP 4 should *precede* STEPS 2 and 3. Accordingly, the *libretto* is *fed* (via *sub* or *super* titles) as the action unfolds. Most modern opera videos employ well timed translation lines which viewers generally regard as very helpful with minimal, if any, distraction.

SECOND COURSE: | "Getting to Know You..."

CONFESSION OF CONTAGION:

My intent, from the very outset of this effort, was to infect you– innocents who may not yet know just how passionately you really love *opera*– with a *bug* similar in *genus* to the one that nailed me (Chapter 2). And, since we are dealing with palatable, but potent, *appetizers*, my recommendations will be few in number but rich in flavor. First-hand experience has consistently shown me that certain works, and specific passages within them, tend to maximize initial exposure to the *organism* which is most likely to produce the condition known as IOAS (Instant Opera Addictive Syndrome). So, by this process, I hereby confess to being a *pusher* and accept all attendant responsibilities in continuing to provide *fixes* as demanded.

A particularly memorable *group high* occurred in 1996 during my course *Carmen and the Italian Verismo*, in which I covered, via lecture and recordings, the enormous influence the great Bizet masterpiece was to have on the then-teenage Italians who would ultimately represent the *last gasp* of standard repertory opera, reaching into the early decades of the 20th century. As a preview of the *veristic* movement to follow, I began with one seminal passage from Act II of Giuseppe Verdi's 1853 *La Traviata**. The result of those moments underscored what I have always viscerally felt, that opera is at its powerful best when it stimulates the heart rather than the brain. Based on the personal experiences of Alexandre Dumas the Younger, *La Traviata* deals with the doomed love of a courtesan (a nice-sounding word usually employed within a setting of wealth– otherwise, far less romantic terms would be substituted) for a young nobleman whose family could not possibly allow that relationship to continue.

---

*La Traviata is usually translated as "The Lost Woman." "The Strayed Woman," however, is probably more literally accurate.

Realizing the utter hopelessness of her plight, following a visit from her beloved's father, the consumptive heroine Violetta begins to write an explanation of her leaving the love-struck Alfred, who enters unexpectedly. Noticing her nervousness, he begins to inquire as she tries to evade her true feelings. As Verdi's orchestra *flits giddily,* in contrast to Violetta's true emotions, her defenses crumble as the orchestra begins to *moan* in a descending scale. No longer able to *play act,* Violetta pours out her soul in music of almost unendurable pathos when, to a build-up of full orchestral palette, she exclaims:

"Amami, Alfredo, amami, quant'io t'amo, Addio!"
(Love me, Alfred, love me as much as I love you, Goodbye!)

The single word "Amami..." is sung three times, first in descent, then on the same note and, finally, thrusting upwards in shattering anguish. Verdi had to be divinely inspired in this brief magic moment.

Describing what the group should expect when I played the recording (a very early 1952 Italian effort starring the then little known Maria Callas), I *set the stage* by informing them that my hands would mimic the orchestra and *flutter* during Violetta's attempt at evasion, that they would then slowly descend when she could restrain her feelings no longer and, in a sweeping semi-circular gesture, I would then slowly raise my arms immediately before her climactic agonizing utterance. That upward motion– somewhere between conducting and *Tai Chi*– stretched almost due horizontal at the very moment the orchestra peaked and the young Callas swelled to the apex. As the ascending final "Amami..." culminated, I heard an extraneous sound that, for a panicky split-second, I feared had somehow invaded the recorded playback. No, it was a collective heave and a muffled exhaling gasp in the chests of my group of elders. Goodness, Gracious! The vast bulk of the group felt, on that elemental level, the great neck-down art form that is so uniquely *opera*: they were *hooked,* and I guess I felt like evangelists must feel when they muster group conversions within some state of stupor.

They reacted to the overwhelming emotions of a wonderful *real person* of *opera* when her creator transcended time from which point his muse would never again look back. I was particularly fortunate to have been his messenger on that day and place.

Within the memory of that still palpable experience, and with the hope of similar addictive *hits* yet to come, here are my recommendations in a specific suggested order. They will not, however, begin with the venerable Verdi but with his younger– by almost a full half century– disciple Giacomo Puccini who would emerge as the man who ran with the Italian opera baton a goodly distance into the 20th century. And, while I never quite give up on potential converts into the wonderful world of *opera*, when one is left unmoved by the essential Puccini after he is properly *offered*, only then do I even begin to think that "...perhaps, *just perhaps* that is, *opera* may not be for you."

Author Matthew Boyden, in noting an oft quoted humorous line that "Wagner's music is better than it sounds" adds, in converse, that "...Puccini's often sounds better than it is." Rest assured that the aspects of Puccini's art which may be debated in such terms will not be on the menu here. The choices are strictly *soul food* though, admittedly, under a new meaning.

♪ - ♪ - ♪ - ♪ - ♪ - ♪ - ♪ - ♪ - ♪ - ♪ - ♪ - ♪ - ♪ - ♪ - ♪ - ♪

So, then, let's get on with the sequential suggestions of "Opera's Regular Guy":

♪ *LA BOHÈME* (The Bohemians), Giacomo Puccini,1858-1924
This 1896 wonder, Puccini's most spontaneous creation, is a work of perennial youth and hope, shattered by early tragedy. The opera is as fresh today as when it premiered under Arturo Toscanini's direction. It is also particularly amenable to setting *transplants*.

♪ *MADAMA BUTTERFLY*, Puccini
Magnificent saga of different cultures and attitudes leading to one

of the most poignant tragedies in all of *opera*, the callous betrayal of the lovingly loyal 15-year-old geisha, known as "Butterfly," by an American Naval Officer at the dawn of the 20th century. The 1904 work, initially a failure, has become one of the most beloved operas worldwide. The pathetic heroine was the composer's favorite, rendering him heartbroken and in tears during the work's creation.

♪ *LA TRAVIATA*, Giuseppe Verdi, 1813-1901
A superb intimate masterpiece (1853) which, with *Rigoletto* two years before, marked a turning point in the composer's development where music and drama were intermingled with far greater depth and cohesive impact. The consumptive heroine Violetta Valery remains one of the most poignant personages in all opera.

♪ *CARMEN*, Georges Bizet, 1838-1875
The most important progenitor of operatic *verismo*, *Carmen* has it all in a vividly gripping and psychological musical stage drama. It's stark realism, ironically, contributed to the initial 1875 failure, tragically followed only three months later by the composer's early death at 37.

♪ *CAVALLERIA RUSTICANA* (Rustic Chivalry), Pietro Mascagni, 1863-1945
This kinetic tale of *real-folk* infidelity and vengeance in late 19th century Sicily placed *verismo* on the operatic map. It is most often offered with its equally extroverted sibling:

♪ *I PAGLIACCI* (The Clowns), Ruggiero Leoncavallo, 1858-1919
Same emotions as above but in *grease-paint*.

And, from column B, the lighter side which may be interspersed with the above:

♪ *THE BARBER OF SEVILLE*, Giaocchino Rossini, 1792-1868
The great comedian of opera serves up the peerless Figaro in this

1816 classic which has been a favorite from the start.   Its effervescence is eternal.

♪ *L'ELISIR D'AMORE* (The Elixir of Love), Gaetano Donizetti, 1797-1848
A hilarious farce of an affable *con man* and a lovable *dunce* as hero. The melodies are infectious in this comic gem.

♪ *DER ROSENKAVALIER* (The Cavalier of the Rose), Richard Strauss, 1864-1949
This uniquely poignant work offers a *bittersweet* mixture of emotions with a magical ending unlike anything else in the genre.

♪ *THE TALES OF HOFFMAN*, Jacques Offenbach, 1819-1880
A fascinating and evocatively macabre work by a German-born master who became as sparklingly French as Champagne itself.

♪ *SHOW BOAT*, Jerome Kern, 1885-1945
Most important work by the *father* of the American stage musical. *Show Boat* rendered the existing *revue* format moot.

♪ *PORGY AND BESS*, George Gershwin, 1898-1937
Wonderful operatic fusion of true American music, incorporating *blues* and *jazz*, by this son of Russian immigrants.

Note: *Hansel and Gretel,* by the *authentic* Engelbert Humperdinck (1854-1921), would be an ideal first live (or video) experience for youngsters. Apropos, a 'hosteler' once added that "... nobody dies" which assumes, of course, that we ignore one Rosina Leckermaul (Sweet-tooth), the *Knusperhexe* (the *Gobbler*-Witch). This magical *kids opera*, indeed, so totally captivated my childhood senses of innocent wonder and fantasy, invaded by trepidation, that they were only partially assuaged by the ultimate triumph of family over fear.

OPERATIC AUDIO/VISUALS: Recommendations

In the post-1948 *analog* LP era, nostalgic memory perhaps retro-seduces us to a huge record store where we chose our treasures from RCA Victor, Columbia, London or Angel and a small handful of sub-strata labels. The reality, however, told a far different tale. In *The Disc Book**, about sixty record companies (representing only one-fourth of the firms with U.S. administrative offices) are specifically listed. One such, as I now refer you back to Chapter 4 with a lingering sense of guilt, was Urania Records, Inc., 40 East 19th Street, New York City– *absolve me already, Igor!* And, as did occur with hundreds of American piano manufacturers, virtually all are long gone. That was then.

This is now. In the post-1982 digital CD era, some of the old names remain: London is still London, RCA's *Nipper* still tends to perk up his ears when *his master's voice* calls and the European Philips and Deutsche Grammophon still breathe, but who knows for how long due to steadily falling sales and bottom-line restructuring? Columbia, however, is now Sony and a group of labels (including Angel) bear the imprint of their huge parent, the Electric and Musical Industries Company (EMI). The fiercer action concerns the smaller labels, established and recent, where reactions are fast and furious in somewhat of a *feeding frenzy* for survival beneath a backdrop of increasingly less enthusiasm for classical music and *opera*. One may soon need the help of that proverbial *scorecard* to keep an accurate tally after the blood clears. Sounds truly grizzly, doesn't it?

Actually, there is much reason for optimism. Really!

♪ - ♪ - ♪ - ♪ - ♪ - ♪ - ♪ - ♪ - ♪ - ♪ - ♪ - ♪ - ♪ - ♪ - ♪ - ♪ - ♪

*David Hall and Abner Levin, Long Player Publications, Stratford Press, New York, 1955.

First, and perhaps foremost, complete opera studio recordings have been in steady decline as they have become prohibitively expensive. Many have been *patchworks* in attempting to accommodate the varied voracious schedules of the shrinking supply of large voiced major singers. (Remember that Sony *Il Trovatore* which was *in process* for three years?) Also, despite wonderful sound engineering, it is increasingly realized that previous releases–many pre-digital– are frequently much superior, again most evident in the area of vocal quality. The trend, then, is to *sanitize* the best of the older efforts in creating a new meaning for *born again*. The differences in sound quality between the *reborn* and the *newborn* is often miraculously minimal. Many of my recommendations, then, are from the rejuvenated gene pool.

A few recent companies, such as the British Nimbus and the Munich based Naxos, produce contemporary digital DDD recording as well as re-mastering the old classics of the 78 RPM era with differing techniques; Naxos, incidentally, has just issued *all* the recordings of the legendary Caruso on the CD format. If *big names* are not of significance, the Naxos line may well approach the ideal– top quality music at a rock bottom price. Covering an enormous breadth of repertory, from ancient music through ultra- modern, Naxos has offered performances of the highest quality, most recorded in Eastern Europe. The company's foray into *opera* has been somewhat less impressive, especially with respect to the larger scaled works such as *Aida*. These discs also include very informative liner notes and the complete operas provide *librettos* which may not, however, have side-by-side English translations.

There are several ways of building a fine quality CD opera collection at particularly affordable cost. Some of the larger record clubs, thanks to the competition of the internet, no longer require a commitment when you get those 11 or 12 for the price of 1– still, it's a good idea to read the fine print. Check out the catalogs of the larger music firms as overstocks and non-sellers are frequently offered far below original price. Sometimes cut-rate takes on a literal meaning where the CD cases are permanently altered via a hole or slit so as to brand the final sale as definitively final (these are, not surprisingly, called *cut-outs*).

Not generally recommended is the purchase of used or, borrowing from the luxury car lexicon, pre-owned CDs. Several stores specialize in this area, the Princeton Record Exchange in New Jersey generally regarded as king. Not as risky as buying recycled vinyl LPs, one must still employ caution as CDs are no more "indestructible" than the "permanent needle" was *permanent*. With this said, a properly cared for disc may be an option if the price warrants but keep in mind that the bargain cut-outs are new despite their plastic surgery.

And, not widely known, the compact disc is recorded from the inside out on the *blank* side, in contrast to the now obsolete LP. Great care, therefore, should be exercised to keep that shiny side free of fingerprints and more serious damage. Also, inquire about proper cleaning of your discs and the laser lens in your player (all the audio and large department stores sell inexpensive products for these purposes). Regarding the CD player, a disc with tiny brushes is very effective in removing dust from the lens and the entire process takes approximately 30 seconds. Many a fine machine has been tossed when only this simple preventive measure was required.

My recommendations will be as specific as possible in terms of cast, orchestra, conductor and year of recording. I will not recommend monaural– pre-stereo c. 1956– recordings though a select few of these have never been equaled, such as the 1953 *Tosca* with Maria Callas, Giuseppe di Stefano and Tito Gobbi, conducted by Victor de Sabata: classics such as this one have properly entered the realm of legend. I will also not suggest live recordings because of highly variable sound quality due to the source, authorized or otherwise, of the transcription. Yet, as with the above mono gem, a few incomparable treasures leap out as glorious exceptions such as that 1961 Met *Turandot* with Nilsson, Corelli, Moffo et al and the matchless conducting of Leopold Stokowski. Unlike the cherished *Tosca*, however, this live legend has always been virtually unobtainable, most unfortunate as the CD sound is far above average. I could not more strongly agree with Matthew Boyden when he regards it as "...the finest performance ever recorded..." and, though difficult to find, "...is worth every effort and any price." This live-capture also serves to transport me back to that magical March 4th original experience at the long gone old Met a nostalgically distant four decades ago. The reverberations of that stentorian few hours, on the other hand, is vividly and eternally ever present to the many who heard that Saturday broadcast but, especially, to the fortunate few of us who were there to witness and cherish.

So, then, let's proceed according to the order suggested for CDs and augmented by the corresponding video for the first six staples. The opera film catalogs, beyond the focus of the most popular repertory favorites, is diffused and contains a *hodgepodge* of live performances (some going back a half-century or more) of highly variable quality. Some, however, are uniquely interesting such as a 1953 *Aida* with the 19-year-old Sophia Loren and the dubbed voice of Renata Tebaldi (personally, this always represented perfection in womanhood for me!). At any rate, I am realistically hopeful that by this point you will already be hooked and will either self-direct or request further addiction assistance which will be gladly furnished. I believe the recommendations to be among the finest available performances, taking into consideration the variables of personal taste. The emphasis on my choices are placed on the side of emotional passion, for only then will the *bite of that bug* tend to be permanent.

Alan Wagner, a New York City opera broadcaster of the late 1950's and 60's, once made a statement that stuck with me: "There is nothing more *boring* than a voice trained far beyond its ability." And, in the promo to "Opera's Regular Guy's" program, one hears that into *The Joy of Opera* "...boredom and stodginess are not admitted once the curtain goes up." "Nosiree," those two never did sneak in, not even once– of this I am quite confident.

CD's	VIDEOS

LA BOHÈME (Puccini)

Freni, Pavarotti, et al	AUSTRALIAN OPERA
Berlin Phil. Orch., KARAJAN	COMPANY
LONDON (2 CDs, 1971)	(superb transplant to the
or	1950's) Highly recommended!
	Cond. SMITH (1993)
	Dir. B. LUHRMANN *or*
Tebaldi, Bergonzi, et al	Freni, Raimondi, et al
St. Cecilia Orch., SERAFIN	La Scala Orch., KARAJAN
LONDON (2 CDs, 1958)	Dir: F. ZEFFIRELLI (1967)
	(Deutsche Grammophon)

NOTE: Avoid a 1999 LONDON CD effort with Bocelli, Frittoli, et al with Mehta conducting. This uninspired recording is disappointing in almost every way.

MADAMA BUTTERFLY (Puccini)

Freni, Pavarotti, et. al	Huang, Troxell, et al
Vienna Phil. Orch., KARAJAN	Cond. CONLON
LONDON (2 CDs, 1974)	Dir. F. MITTERAND (1995)
or	(Sony) presented by Martin
De Los Angeles, Björling, et al	Scorsese
Rome Opera Orch., SANTINI	
EMI (2 CDs, 1959)	

LA TRAVIATA (Verdi)

Sutherland, Bergonzi, Merrill, et al	Domingo, Stratas, MacNeil, et al
Florence May Festival Orch.,	Cond. LEVINE
PRITCHARD LONDON	Dir. F. ZEFFIRELLI (1982)
(2 CDs, 1962)	
or	
Gheorghiu, Lopardo, et al	
Covent Garden Orch., SOLTI	
LONDON (2 CDs, 1992)	

CD's	VIDEOS

CARMEN (Bizet)

CD's	VIDEOS
Price, Corelli, Merrill, et al Vienna Phil. Orch., KARAJAN RCA (3 CDs, 1963)	Migenes-Johnson, Domingo, et al Cond. MAAZEL Dir. F. ROSI COLUMBIA-TRISTAR (1984)

NOTE: This CD performance, the most thrilling *Carmen* ever recorded, is decidedly not the choice of Francophiles. To each his own and this is my book.

CAVALLERIA RUSTICANA (Mascagni) and *I PAGLIACCI* (Leoncavallo)

CD's	VIDEOS
Corelli, De Los Angeles, et al SANTINI **and** Corelli, Gobbi, Amara, et al(MATACIC)	Domingo, Stratas, et al Cond. PRETRE Dir. F. ZEFFIRELLI PHILIPS (1984/1985)

NOTE: The above two operas should be purchased in a set- EMI (2 CDs, 1963 and 1961)

CDs Only

THE BARBER OF SEVILLE (Rossini)	Servile, Ganassi, Vargas, et al Failoni Chamber Orch., HUMBURG NAXOS (1993), complete or excerpts
L'ELISIR D'AMORE (Donizetti)	Sutherland, Pavarotti, et al English Chamber Orch., BONYNGE LONDON (2 CDs, 1969)
DER ROSENKAVALIER (Strauss)	Te Kanawa, von Otter, Leech, et al Dresden State Orch., HAITINK EMI (1991) - excerpts (1 CD)

CDs Only

THE TALES OF HOFFMAN (Offenbach)	Domingo, Sutherland, Bacquier, et al Orchestra. of Suisse Romande, BONYNGE LONDON (2 CDs, 1971)
SHOW BOAT (Kern)	Hadley, von Stade, Stratas, Hubbard, et al London Sinfonietta, McGLINN EMI (3 CDs, 1988)
PORGY AND BESS (Gershwin)	White, Haymon, Blackwell, et al London Phil. Orch., RATTLE EMI (3 CDs, 1988)

Some sources for Opera CDs and Videos in addition to the large retail stores:

DAEDALUS:	www.salemusic.com	800-395-2665
FACETS:	www.facets.org	800-331-6197
BEL CANTO SOCIETY	www.belcantosociety.org	800-347-5056
MOVIES UNLIMITED	www.moviesunlimited.com	800-4-MOVIES
Amazon.com (new/used)	www.amazon.com	800-201-7575

You are now vividly poised to continue the long but wondrous journey on the *yellow brick road* (alas! not *brewery*) to the *Oz* of *opera* without encountering that *slickster* behind the curtain at the finish line. The magic can be infinite: that glorious genius Mozart, more Verdi (*Rigoletto* and *Aida*), the melodramatic Puccini (*Tosca* and *Turandot*), *Bel Canto*, French and Russian *dressings* (especially the very *soul* of the people in Mussorgsky's Boris Godunov), the evocative mystics Claude Debussy and Frederick Delius, and on, and endlessly on, until we ultimately reach the summit of operatic music drama in Wagner's* *Tristan and Isolde* and Verdi's *Otello*, the most profound psychological penetration of all where the composer met his idol Shakespeare on consecrated common ground.

Bon Voyage! And, once again, if you feel as if you're drifting along the way, call for assistance at susbrody@aol.com.

*Richard Wagner (1813-1883), arguably the colossus of *opera*, is musically and philosophically complex to put it mildly. Many people deny themselves his magnificent music because the person was particularly unpleasant. So important, however, is he that we must find a way to separate man from musician. In keeping with the purpose of this primer, I will not serve you the full Wagnerian course when the nature of the *food* may be unfamiliar. Orchestral excerpts only will be suggested here and I will recommend two performances on one CD each though I suggest both (there is an overlap of one excerpt). There are many single CDs in the catalog of instrumental music of this giant.

London Symphony Orchestra, Leopold Stokowski, conductor.
LONDON (rec. 1966 and 1972) - #421 020-2 LC
(this CD was released under the budget category called "Weekend Classics")

Berlin Philharmonic Orchestra, Herbert von Karajan, conductor.
DEUTSCHE GRAMMOPHON (rec. 1984) - #D 108695

EPILOGUE: "Quo Vadis?"

> "Where the telescope ends,
> the microscope begins..."
> *–Victor Hugo*

The future of *opera* should not be predicted through the current activities of opera companies, large and small, in marketing their wares to the perennially eager *opera goer*. No, the essential viability of the great art form will primarily emanate, as it always has, from its root system. And so, after our diverse meandering journey, we have returned full circle to Homer and the passionate passing of the torch through time.

Whether folk song passed through in Ancient Greece, or wide eyed Gypsy children wondrously absorbing their heritage in dance, tradition ever expands its web. More limited, but thrilling nonetheless, were the feelings of the children of the 20th century's early years when they were given the honor of *cranking up* the old *Gramophone* from which Caruso, McCormack or Galli-Curci would soon enter their parlors as those scratchy sounds would be passed through as well. These *children* are hopefully glowing in their *twilight* now as so many have related to me, in my courses, of their last desire to operatically touch their grandchildren as they missed that chance with their own. As it always seems to do, life again interfered.

And, in this venue, I must confess that I speak to you as somewhat of a hypocrite. Passing it through, my children always heard music in their home, whether live from several pianos or recorded via several turntables; yet, I never took a direct approach save sending my 12-year-old grand-daughter the lovely book *Aida* by Leontyne Price plus a CD of highlights from that all encompassing Verdi work. No *lightning strike* nor any other response as yet. Her father, a splendid guitarist, is a *rocker* (in the very best sense of the word I best add).

As this work drew to its close, a most fortuitous serendipity* appeared in a newspaper article entitled "Classical rocks." ** Though the piece focuses on the state of the symphony orchestra in America, the word *opera* can be safely substituted with absolutely no alteration of concept. Peralta points out that of the nation's five major orchestras (New York, Philadelphia, Cleveland, Chicago, and Boston) only the latter is not facing a deficit. The main thrust of the article, however, deals with how the local Jacksonville Symphony Orchestra intends to function with its cumulative deficit of almost $2.5 million, not to speak of the more than a few empty seats in the auditorium. Of great importance is the fact that about half of their subscribers are over 65 years of age, while those under 45 comprise a somewhat paltry 15 percent. A 2002 Knight Foundation study of 15 U.S. orchestras found that a full half of adults "expressed a negative preference for attending classical music concerts." (Again, please feel free to substitute the word *opera* for classical music). To try to cleanse the stagnant status quo, the JSO will perform "The Music of Led Zeppelin: A Rock Symphony." Time will tell whether this daring *crossover* jump will clear the hurdle– the delicacy here has always been in the tenuous balance of box office receipts and artistic integrity. The dramatic cover photo shows a diversely bold quartet of *rockers* horizontally hoisting aloft a panicked tuxedo wearing French Hornist. JSO's attempt in this venture is to excavate beyond the soon retiring *boomers* to the layer of *their* offspring, or the 20 to 40 year old age group. There is little doubt that *opera*, as it already has clearly signaled, will inevitably follow along this road as well. *Transplanted opera* by setting has occasionally succeeded, provided that the singing is of the front rank. In the end, one can make the case, with Corelli, that *opera* is primarily a *vocal* art form. Others, however, may make an opposite argument so, as usual, *time* will be the final arbiter.

---

*French. - An agreeable gift not overtly sought (derives from the fairy tale *The Three Princes of Serendip*).
**Eyder Peralta, *The Florida Times-Union* (Jacksonville), September 22, 2004.

A pervasive puzzlement* may soon be clarified: if the Symphony succeeds with "...A Rock Symphony" and the Opera House *hits* in its own such counterpart, will the newly wooed youth come back to hear a couple of *older dudes* whose names are Beethoven and Verdi?

*"Buona Fortuna!"***

---

*This word existed before being rendered immortal by King Monkut of Siam.
**Italian. - *Good luck*: (in Amilcare Ponchielli's *La Gioconda*, the villain Barnaba sings these words to spine chilling sardonic effect).

BASIC OPERA GLOSSARY

ALTO - It. **high** - a voice category in mixed chorus, not used in opera.

ARIA - It. **air** - a song for solo voice.

BARCAROLLE - 'boatman's song' using a swaying rhythm.

BARITONE - Gr. - **deep tone** - male voice lying between tenor and bass.

BASSO - It. **low** - lowest male voice in opera.

BEL CANTO - It. - **beautiful song** - refers to a specific vocal style, most popular in the early 19th century in the works of Rossini, Donizetti and Bellini. Florid singing prevalent.

CABALETTA - It. **gallop** - a short, fast finale following an aria.

CASTRATO - It. **castrated**. A surgically induced male soprano in vogue during the 17th and 18th centuries by which the singer had the power of a male and the sound of a female.

COLORATURA - A highly ornamented vocal style usually associated with the high soprano voice (leggiera). It is not accurate to define a voice by this technique.

CONTRALTO - It. **contrasting the alto** - the lowest of female voices in opera.

COUNTER-TENOR - modern day vocal equivalent of the castrato; a very high male voice.

FALSETTO - It. **false** - a vocal technique by which male voices could approximate females.

HELDENTENOR - G. - **heroic tenor** - a powerful voice suited for the heavier roles such as required in the works of Richard Wagner.

IGARROPHANT - contraction of the three mentioned entities of Chapter 5; on the endangered species list, these are frequently found in and around concert halls and opera houses.

LEGATO - It. **bound together** - a smooth singing line without detachment of tones.

LEITMOTIF - G. **leading motive** - musical themes representing characters or events.

LIBRETTO - It. **little book** - the text from which operas are composed.

MEZZO SOPRANO - It. **middle soprano** - female voice between a light soprano and contralto.

OPERA - It. **work** or **works** from the Latin **opus**.

OPERA BUFFA - It. **comic opera**.

OPERA COMIQUE - Fr. **comic opera** but relates to a form including spoken dialogue.

OVERTURE - Fr. **opening** - the passage which precedes the opera.

PIANISSIMO - It. **very softly** - singing in accord with the aforementioned directions.

PORTAMENTO - It. **carrying** - singing one note to a distant one, barely touching those in between.

PRIMA DONNA - It. **first lady** - the leading female cast member.

PRIMO UOMO - It. **first man** - this category usage has become virtually obsolete.

RECITATIVE - a semi-verbal narrative which precedes an aria.

RUBATO - It. to **rob/steal** - tempo slightly delayed or accelerated for dramatic effect.

SINGSPIEL - G. **song play** - a German form of light opera including spoken dialogue, the German counterpart of Opera Comique. Glorified in many of the works of Mozart.

SOPRANO - It. **over**, **above** - from highest to lowest - leggiera, lyric, dramatic, mezzo and contralto.

SPINTO - It. **pushed** - a technique that can 'push' some voices, not to strain, but to enhanced dramatic effect. Term primarily used for some sopranos and tenors.

TENOR - Lat. **to hold/support** - in the pre-opera years, the tenor held a firm line in the Church. Only later did this high male voice become the 'matinee idol'. From highest to lowest, leggiero, lyric and dramatic.

TESSITURA - It. **texture** - the predominant range of a voice or the music sung.

TRILL - a **rapid alternation** of a note and the one above it.

VERISMO - It. **very truthful** - realism and real people in opera, frequently dealing with violent situations.

VIBRATO - It. **vibrating** - a throbbing oscillation of tone which is far more popular in Italy than in England or America.

ZARZUELA - a sprightly Spanish vocal stage musical with spoken dialogue.

APPENDIX A

Last Millennium B.C. - Evidence now indicates that the Ancient Greek plays were sung, with musical accompaniment, and that Homer was a singer from a long line of folk vocalists.

Early Background - In Europe, during the Middle Ages (500 - 1500 A.D.), church *mystery plays* and simple dramas were performed in some inns.   In the mid-Renaissance (approximately 1400 -1550 A.D.), the *comedies of masks* were performed by strolling troupes, frequently to musical accompaniment.

Last Years of 16th C. - Musical dramas were performed at the Florentine Court for the nobility. In 1597, Peri (amateur musician) and Rinuccini (amateur poet) collaborated on musical settings to the classic Greek tragedies and the first *operas* emerged– *Dafne* and *Euridice*.

17th C. - Claudio Monteverdi (1567-1643), opera's first man of genius, would influence all who followed. Works included *Orfeo* (1607) and *The Coronation of Poppea* (1643). His pupil Cavalli opened the first public opera house in Venice in 1637.   In France, Lully and Rameau were preeminent as was Purcell in England; *Dido and Aeneas* (1689) endures as a masterpiece. In Germany, *opera* evolved later due to a slower separation from the church. Though operatic characters veered away from mythology toward human beings, they still had to be *heroic* humans.

18th C. - Center stage for the *prima donna* and the *castrato,* primarily in the music of Handel (1685-1759). An early comic masterpiece was Pergolesi's *La Serva Padrona* (The Maid Mistress) of 1733.   Gluck (1714-1787) , known as *the great reformer*, saved *opera* from its out of control singers who would change the composer's music at will. Gluck's *Orfeo and Euridice* (1762) remains the oldest serious work still performed in the repertories of opera houses. The century closed with the glorious Mozart (1756-1791).

19th C. - Beethoven's *Fidelio* was the titan's only dip in the operatic pool. Weber (1786-1826) was the pioneer of true German Romantic Opera with *Der Freischutz* (1821). In Italy, there were thirty glorious years of *Bel Canto* (Rossini, Donizetti, Bellini and young Verdi). In France, there were *a few good men* and Bizet (1838-1875). In Russia, the *volcano* erupted and *folk opera* proliferated in Eastern Europe and in Spain. Verdi (1813-1901) and Wagner (1813-1883) would revolutionize dramatic opera. Italian *verismo* (realism) was born in the last decade as Puccini would soon dominate post-Verdi Italian opera.

20th C. - R. Strauss (1864-1949) is the *last gasp* of German repertory opera. Puccini (1858-1924) lowers the curtain of standard repertory opera with the unfinished *Turandot* and *experimentation* follows. Joplin, Kern and Gershwin plant American seeds.

21st C. - ??? - Excursions into *crossover* appears inevitable for the future survival of the art form in attracting younger audiences. Time will judge the success of these ventures.

APPENDIX B

OPERA NEWS *a publication of*

The Metropolitan Opera Guild, Inc.

654 Madison Avenue   New York 21, New York   TEmpleton 8-8500

December 23, 1958

Dear Mr. Brody:

Thank you for your remarks of December 14;
I wish that it were within the scope of OPERA NEWS
to publish them. Not having heard Mr. Corelli, I am
afraid I have no personal opinion on the subject.

Sincerely yours,

Frank Merkling

Frank Merkling

FM:rb

APPENDIX C

CAPITOL RECORDS, INC.

1730 BROADWAY AT 55TH • NEW YORK 19, N. Y. • PLAZA 7-7470

January 13, 1959

Mr. Gerald Brody
1850 81st Street
Brooklyn 14, New York

Dear Mr. Brody:

Thank you sincerely for your enthusiastic praise of our product.
Mr. Corelli's name is familiar to me and to several of my
colleagues. Though I can offer you nothing conclusive, I can
assure you that he is not going unnoticed.

I am enclosing our newest catalogues. Thank you for your
interest in our recorded music.

With all best wishes, I am

Yours sincerely,

Jack Romann
CAPITOL RECORDS

JR:ros
Enclosures

APPENDIX D
Basic Bibliography

Introduction: As our journey just concluded with discussion of the nebulous and tenuous future of *opera* as our nascent century moves on, a truly sobering experience just occurred which is relevantly revealing. Having some time to spend while a photocopy job was being run (the final draft of this effort), I ambled into the adjacent bookstore of one of the largest chains in the country. While being escorted to the 'music section', the very pleasant salesperson informed me, en route, not to "...expect too much..." in the way of *opera*. The one designated wooden bookcase measured what looked like ten feet in width by seven feet in height. With the exception of one thin paperback on the *proper technique for singers*, there was not a solitary work related to *opera*, its history or any other facet of its very being. I remain stunned by this yet it begs a story which, I guess, I'm currently relating. My memory riveted back to the mid-1950's (same bookstore chain, incidentally) when, at the least, that *entire* bookcase would have been needed to house the myriad volumes on *opera* which would dourly stare us down. Clearly, that bookcase of 1955 had to descend from the 19th century as it surely could not possibly have had any involvement in the siring of this one in the 21st.

♪ - ♪ - ♪ - ♪ - ♪ - ♪ - ♪ - ♪ - ♪ - ♪ - ♪ - ♪ - ♪ - ♪ - ♪ - ♪ - ♪

The majority of musical books use terms which assume a familiarity that many readers may not possess. First and foremost, then, a basic dictionary is essential. There are a good few available but my choice is an inexpensive and highly compact, yet surprisingly comprehensive, little edition measuring only 4" x 5½" yet it manages to contain 237 well devised pages including brief bios, charts, definitions, and a *time line* of significant composers from Guillaume de Machaut (b. 1300) through Philip Glass, born 637 years later.

> Hal Leonard, <u>Pocket Music Dictionary</u>,
> Hal Leonard Publishing, 1993.
> (app. $5)

Recommendations for Basic/Intermediate Levels:

*****HIGHEST RECOMMENDATION (*a must for most*)–

> Matthew Boyden, <u>The Rough Guide to Opera</u>,
> (3rd edition), Rough Guides Ltd.,
> (Dist. by the Penguin Group), London, 2002
> Paperback (735 pages), (app. $25)

This is a brilliantly devised, comprehensive effort which is also a delight to read. It provides, in the most helpful formatting imaginable, the chronological historical progression of composers and their operas, highly concise synopses of plots (some minimally adequate and no substitute for reading the stories of the operas) and recommendations of CD recordings, both vintage and contemporary. Highly informative features are beautifully interspersed throughout the work which also includes photos, sketches, summarized discussions of major singers, and conductors (current and past) and a glossary. The writing is also humorous and, despite its grand scope, it never even hints at the haughty condescension which too frequently infects many books dealing with this subject. Rarely is one offered such a pleasant package as this one. Note: Being an English publication, certain differences exist such as the London label in this country being Decca in the U.K. My only *nit-pik* is the absence, in the "Directory of singers," of the incomparable American dramatic soprano Eileen Farrell (1920 - 2002) though Boyden clearly notes that the inclusions were primarily based on the frequency of mention in the recommended CDs. Indeed, and so regrettably, Farrell was virtually non-existent on complete studio recordings yet the voice was truly monumental and her treasured 1957 EMI gem (originally released here on an Angel LP) with the Philharmonia Orchestra under Thomas Schippers, remains one of the colossal vocal achievements of the 20th century and belongs on Mt. Olympus' honor roll in Herculean operatic eternity.

Two popular books can be recommended *if* the above work is not obtainable:

> David Pogue and Scott Speck, <u>Opera for Dummies</u>,
> Hungry Minds, Inc. (w. EMI), 1997.

and,

> Fred Plotkin, <u>Opera 101</u>, Hyperion Books, 1994.

VINTAGE CLASSICS: (experience the *thrill* of finding these treasures in *recycled* bookstores).

> <u>Kobbe's Complete Opera Book</u> (edited by the Earl of Harewood),
> G. P. Putnam's Sons, 1972 (single volume, 1,262 pages).

Note: Later editions comprise two volumes and discuss well over 250 operas. In this seminal work, in print since 1922, operas are analyzed with musical annotations and the narrative, in elegant flowery style, almost approaches poetry.

> <u>Milton Cross' Complete Stories of the Great Operas</u>,
> Doubleday, 1952.

Note: The work includes sketches, history, *tips* on enjoying *opera* and bibliography.

> Wallace Brockway and Herbert Weinstock, <u>The World of Opera</u>,
> Pantheon Books, 1962 (includes *Annals of Performance of Operas*).

Note: A superb, scholarly chronological journey through the entire history of *opera*– a universally lauded effort.

> <u>The Opera Reader</u> (edited by Louis Biancolli),
> McGraw-Hill, 1953.

Note: Incisive synopses of operas with critical reviews and opinion.

A personal favorite–

John Briggs, <u>Requiem for a Yellow Brick Brewery</u>,
(A History of the Metropolitan Opera), Little, Brown and Company, 1969.

Note: A fascinating nostalgic history of the rise, decline and fall (literally) of the great *Old Met* on 39th Street and Broadway in New York City; the *grand house* lived from 1883 through 1966 in glory, distress and ultimate destruction. Wonderful photos included in this bittersweet masterpiece of a book. (Again, *Yellow Brick Brewery* was a derisive name given to the *old house* by a rival impresario.)

APPENDIX E
Bravo Buffo

Many frequent opera going fans well recall live experiences at theatres where things did not go quite as planned. One personal memory was when, in *Il Trovatore*, only the totally detached handle emerged from the sheath and Ted Buchter related how a pre-performance worker left the vacuum cleaner on stage as the curtain went up and, as if part of the plot, a costumed individual gracefully scampered in and retrieved it with dramatic aplomb.

The following range from humorous *faux-pas* (lit. missteps), through indelible *ad-libs* to downright *disaster*. Let us begin on the simple side and then descend shockingly downhill:

♪ "Every theatre is a lunatic asylum and opera is the ward for incurables." (attributed to a friend of Franz Liszt).

♪ "If you never attended an opera and the following chapters should create in you a desire to do so, please stay long enough to enjoy an intermission! It's often the best part of the evening." *My Favorite Intermissions*, Victor Borge with Robert Sherman, Dorset Press, New York, 1971.

♪ During Rudolph Bing's regime, each act of one performance of *Tristan and Isolde* had a different tenor lead due to a particularly bad evening of vocal shortcomings. Though unplanned, this surely represented the original version of *The Three Tenors*.

♪ A decision was made in a British production of *Don Giovanni* to place a microphone in the heavily tiled lavatory to add an eerie reverberance to the *hell scene* in the final act. Indeed it became *hell* when that particular facility was not deemed *off limits*. As the *stone statue* appeared with Mozart's ominous chords, another sound was superimposed- the clarion flushing of a toilet!

♪ *Tosca* is probably the most disaster prone opera in the standard repertory. In this most accepted version among many, the abrasive *prima donna* at a New York City Opera production, was less than gracious to the stage staff.

Jumping from the roof of the *Castel Sant' Angelo* to her death with the words "O Scarpia, avanti a Dio" (Oh Scarpia, before God), this Tosca promptly reappeared. Instead of the customary layers of mattresses, a trampoline was substituted. The revenge of the stage crew was complete!

♪ One of several versions of this live performance classic. During Verdi's *Aida*, one of the stage elephants, in full view, was less than discreet - those within ear shot clearly heard the inimitable conductor Sir Thomas Beecham mutter above the orchestra "...shocking manners, but what a critic"!

♪ In the early years of the 20th century, the Czech tenor Leo Slezak was one of the great interpreters of the title role in Wagner's *Lohengrin*. In the opera, the noble knight appears and leaves via a boat drawn by a graceful swan. In a Viennese performance, Slezak missed the exiting vessel and asked, in stentorian voice, "when does the next swan leave?" The spontaneous audience response completed the now legendary improvised stage drama. (Note: this anecdote is frequently, but inaccurately, attributed to "the Great Dane" Lauritz Melchior.)

AFTERGLOW

Opera is unique in enabling us to hear the expression of emotion by more than one person at the same time. Let's conclude with a vivid supporting experiment which made an indelible impression on me some fifty years ago when it was broadcast as part of a Metropolitan Opera intermission feature.

The "Sextet" from Gaetano Donizetti's *Lucia di Lammermoor* is, arguably, the greatest ensemble piece in all of opera, in which all six characters simultaneously vent their despair with profound effect. Listen, without interruption, to one of any number of fine recordings, preferably first reviewing the words from the text.

When the magic of that moment finally begins to ebb, try to imagine (it was demonstrated when first aired) the cacophonous chaos of those same six people *speaking* at the same time.

♪ - ♪ - ♪ - ♪ - ♪ - ♪ - ♪ - ♪ - ♪ - ♪ - ♪ - ♪ - ♪ - ♪ - ♪ - ♪

In 1953, my parents were about to purchase an RCA boxed LP set of *Aida* with Beniamino Gigli, et al (originally issued on 78) when Sam Goody himself– yes, he *personally* attended to business at his original New York City Store– suggested that they consider a newly released London recording, in better sound, which had young singers who "...should go far." The lead artists in the roles of Aida and Radames were Renata Tebaldi and Mario del Monaco. We listened to you and thank you, Mr. Goody.

♪ - ♪ - ♪ - ♪ - ♪ - ♪ - ♪ - ♪ - ♪ - ♪ - ♪ - ♪ - ♪ - ♪ - ♪ - ♪

Not one comma of this effort, let alone a fully developed word, would have seen the *white-of-page* if it were not for the unwavering support of my soul-spouse Susan D. Brody who elevated the *guilt trip* to a *velvet art* in insisting that I had something different and important to say which had to be shared. During the transcription (she had barely become computer literate), some of my impatience must have bordered on abuse but she absorbed it all in her usual lovingly gentle fashion. Thank you, Sweetheart!

–"Opera's Regular Guy"

Index

About the Author

Gerry Brody, a performing pianist since childhood, was bitten by the opera bug in his mid-teens. Over time, he has amassed an enormous vocal collection of vintage vinyls which he shares with his listeners via his popular long-running weekly radio program *The Joy of Opera*: in this venue, he is an admitted dinosaur and is particularly proud of it. Mr. Brody is also very active in teaching courses in Opera Appreciation for the Continuing Education Programs of Eckerd College and Stetson University as well as conducting seminars incorporating opera videos and live piano augmentation. Gerry resides in St. Augustine, Florida, with his wife, Susan.

ISBN 141208994-8

9 781412 089944